HORRIBLE HISTORIES
MOVIE
ROTTEN ROMANS

Also includes
CUT-THROAT CELTS

Terry Deary
Illustrated by **Martin Brown**

■ **SCHOLASTIC**

Scholastic Children's Books,
Euston House, 24 Eversholt Street,
London NW1 1DB, UK

A division of Scholastic Ltd
London ~ New York ~ Toronto ~ Sydney ~ Auckland
Mexico City ~ New Delhi ~ Hong Kong

Horrible Histories: Rotten Romans first published by Scholastic Ltd, 1994
Horrible Histories: Cut-throat Celts first published by Scholastic Ltd, 1997
This edition published by Scholastic Ltd, 2019

ISBN 978 1407 19705 0

Printed and bound in the UK by CPI Group Ltd, Croydon, CR0 4YY

2 4 6 8 10 9 7 5 3

www.scholastic.co.uk
horriblehistories.movie

Contents
Rotten Romans

Contents
Cut-throat Celts

ROTTEN ROMANS

History can be horrible. Horribly hard to learn. The trouble is it keeps on changing. In maths, two and two is usually four – and in science water is always made up of hydrogen and oxygen.

But in history things aren't that simple. In history a "fact" is sometimes not a fact at all. Really it's just someone's "opinion". And opinions can be different for different people.

For example … you probably think your teacher is more horrible than the cold cabbage and custard you had for school dinner. That's your opinion. But teacher's mum probably thinks he's sweeter than tea with six sugars. That's her opinion.

You could both be right – or both be wrong…

See what I mean? Both right, both wrong!

Of course, honest answers like these don't get you gold stars. No! Teachers will try to tell you there are "right" and "wrong" answers even if there aren't.

There are worse things than horrible history. Want to know what? Teachers' jokes are more horrible than the **Tower of London Torture Chamber...**

So, history can be horrible. But when you find the real truth about the past you can suddenly discover it's **horribly fascinating**. Everyone loves a good murder story – history is full of them, like the murder of Julius Caesar. Blood all over the place

And there are war stories, thrillers, horror stories and comedies. That's the sort of history you'll find in this book. With a bit of luck you might even horrify your teacher!

Rotten Roman Timeline

753 BC

Roman legend says Rome was founded by **Romulus**. The truth is that the early Romans were farmers living in a region called **Latium**.

FEEL LIKE FOUNDING AN EMPIRE?

509 BC

The Romans are fed up with their cruel king, **Tarquin**. They throw him out and rule themselves (that's called a Republic).

TARQUIN TARQUIN TARQUIN OUT OUT OUT!

IT WAS A DAFT NAME ANYWAY

264 BC

First of the Punic Wars against the great enemy, Carthage (in North Africa).

Result: **Rome 1 Carthage 0**.

218 BC

Hannibal of Carthage attacks Rome with the help of elephants. He can't capture Rome but rampages round Italy terrorizing people.

202 BC

Scipio takes charge of the Roman Army and beats Hannibal. **Rome 2 Carthage 0**. The Roman farmers take over more and more land till they have the whole of Italy.

146 BC

Third War to wipe Carthage out for ever. Game, set and match to Rome! The Romans get to like the idea of conquering

people! They start on the rest of the world.

130 BC

By now the Romans have conquered Greece and most of Spain.

100 BC

Julius Caesar is born.

59 BC

Julius Caesar becomes Consul for the first time.

55 BC

Julius Caesar invades **Britain** for the first time because (he says) **a)** the Belgae of south Britain are helping the Gauls of north France to rebel against the Romans, and **b)** there is a wealth of tin, copper and lead to be found in Britain.

44 BC

Julius Caesar is elected dictator for life – then **murdered!**

AD 43

Claudius gives orders for the invasion of Britain ... again!

I'M OFF!

12

AD 60

One tribe, the Iceni, rebel. Queen **Boudicca** leads them in massacres of Romans. Roman General Paulinus defeats her and **she poisons herself**.

AD 80

Julius Agricola completes the invasion (except for the Picts in Scotland).

AD 84

Agricola beats the Picts at Mons Graupius in Scotland.

AD 122

Hadrian starts building a wall across northern England to **keep out** the Picts.

13

AD 235–285

Fifty-year period with over 20 Roman emperors mainly because they keep getting **murdered**.

AD 313

Emperor Constantine allows Christian worship.

AD 380

Christianity becomes official religion of Rome.

AD 401

Roman troops are being withdrawn from Britain to defend Rome.

AD 410

Barbarian tribes from Germany begin attacks on the empire and Rome itself.

AD 476

The last Roman emperor of the western empire is forced to retire.

AD 1453

The empire of the east falls to the Turks. **End of the Roman Empire**.

I'VE NEVER HAD TO PILLAGE ANYTHING THIS BIG BEFORE

The Rotten Roman Army

In the year AD 43 the Romans invaded Britain. The Roman Army didn't run all of Roman Britain. Once they'd won the battles they moved on to fight somewhere else. Towns were built in the beaten bits with Roman lords in charge. Just in case the Britons felt like revolting, the Romans let retired Roman soldiers settle in the land outside the towns – a circle of trusted men to warn of danger. And, if the battered Brits did give trouble then the army could get back quickly to help by marching along the new Roman roads.

Your teachers will tell you all about the legions and what they wore and how they lived. But they don't know everything.

TEST YOUR TEACHER...

Ask your teacher these questions.
Can they get more than 5 out of
10? Can you?

If you were a Roman soldier...
1 What would you wear under your
leather kilt?
a) nothing
b) underpants
c) fig leaves

2 Where would you drive on the
Roman roads?
a) on the right
b) down the centre
c) on the left

3 How long would you have to stay in the army once you joined?

a) 25 years

b) 5 years

c) the rest of your life

I'M A CENTURIAN CENTURIAN

4 Who could you marry?

a) your granny

b) no one

c) a Roman

5 Who paid for your uniform, weapons, food and burial?
a) the emperor
b) your granny
c) you paid for them yourself out of your wages

6 How tall did you have to be?
a) over 1.8 metres
b) between 1.6 and 1.8 metres
c) tall enough to touch your toes

7 What would you use instead of toilet paper?
a) a sponge on the end of a stick
b) your tunic
c) the daily newspaper

8 Your spear (pilum) had a 60-cm metal head that would snap off after it hit something. Why?

a) so the enemy couldn't pick up the spear and throw it back

b) so you could put the metal head in your pocket when you were marching

c) because the Roman armourers couldn't make the heads stay on

9 Why was one Roman Centurion called "Give me another"?

a) because he liked his soldiers to sing as they marched. When they'd finished one song he'd call out, "Give me another!"

b) because he was greedy. After eating a pig's head he'd cry out, "Give me another!"

c) because he cruelly beat his soldiers so hard he smashed his canes and had to call out,

"GIVE ME ANOTHER!"

10 Why would the army doctor not notice your screams as he treated your wounds?

a) because he enjoyed making you suffer

b) because he was trained to carry on without caring about a soldier's cries

c) because the Romans only employed deaf men as doctors

Answers

1b. 2c (But they often barged straight down the middle of town streets in their chariots. They marched there too, trampling anyone who got in the way with their hob–nailed boots!). **3a. 4b** (But they often had wives outside of the camp). **5c. 6b.** (But this rule was sometimes broken when the army was desperate for men … and the men who were too small might still have to work for the army even if they couldn't fight). **7a** (And you'd share it with everyone else in the public toilets! Sometimes you'd use a lump of moss, though, and that would be flushed away). **8a. 9c. 10b.**

The rottenly clever Roman Army

The Romans were the best army in the ancient world because they used something their enemies didn't. The Romans used their brains! Are you as brainy?

Here are some problems the Romans overcame. What would you have done if you'd faced these problems?

I Julius Caesar had a land army in Gaul (northern France). When the Veneti tribe there rebelled, they captured two Roman messengers and sailed off with them. Caesar quickly had ships built and followed. The Veneti were excellent sailors but poor fighters. Caesar needed a weapon that would stop the

Veneti ships from sailing off while Roman soldiers climbed aboard. There was no gunpowder (for cannon or bullets). What simple (but very successful) weapon did the Romans make?

2 After the British Queen Boudicca was beaten, the Romans were able to move into the fenlands of East Anglia. The grass was rich but the land was very wet. If the Romans tried to wade through the swamps, the local tribes ambushed them. Then a new general arrived from Italy's Pontine marshes. He showed the soldiers how to get through swamps without wading up to their waists in water. What did he teach them?

3 In the early days of the Roman Republic, the Romans came up against the Greek king, Pyrrhus. The Greeks would go into battle led by elephants.

The elephants would charge at the Romans, trample them and send them running. But the Romans learned quickly. At the battle of Beneventum they found a way to face an elephant charge ... and win! What would you do?

4 Some of the young men in the conquered lands did not want to fight in the Roman Army. It meant leaving their homes, farms and families to fight (and maybe die) in some distant corner of the world. The young men cut off the thumb of their right hand so they couldn't hold a sword. If they couldn't hold a sword then they wouldn't be expected to fight in the Roman Army. The Roman generals realized that all of these thumbless young men were trying to outwit them. What was their way of stopping this?

5 One day, Emperor Hadrian went to the public baths where his skin was carefully cleaned by slaves with scrapers. He saw an old man rubbing his back against a column. The old man was one of Hadrian's old soldiers. Hadrian asked why he was rubbing himself against the marble. The old man said it was because he couldn't afford a slave with a scraper. Hadrian gave the man slaves and money. BUT ... the next day the public baths were full of old men rubbing their backs against the marble! They were scrounging for a Hadrian handout! What would you do if you were Hadrian?

Answers

1 The Romans fixed hooked knives on to the ends of long poles. As they neared the Veneti ships, the Romans slashed the enemy ropes and sails to stop them sailing. They then climbed aboard the Veneti boats and captured the sailors. The leaders were executed and the sailors sold for slavery.

2 How to use stilts! They were a great success at first. Eventually the tribes of the fens learned to knock the Romans off the stilts and stab them as they fell. Ah, well, it seemed like a brilliant idea at the time!

3 The Roman front line split in two. The elephants charged harmlessly through the line.

They were too clumsy for the drivers to stop and turn. The helpless riders just kept going to the back of the Roman Army, where there were special troops waiting with long, sharp spears. They jabbed the elephants until the maddened creatures turned round and charged back again. The elephants flattened the Greek army, who weren't expecting them!

4 Cut off their heads! Anyone trying to avoid army service was sentenced to death. The young men soon learned this new law and decided to fight – possible death in war was better than certain death by execution. The Romans also branded or tattooed unwilling soldiers – if the soldier deserted, then he would have trouble hiding the fact that he was supposed to be in the army.

> **5** Hadrian simply told the old men to rub each other's backs!

Make the punishment fit the crime

If you think punishments at school are hard, then how would you like to have been in the Roman Army? The barbarian armies charged at the Romans like bulls at a matador – and we know who usually wins that contest. The Roman Army had "discipline". They did what they were told, every time. And if they didn't do as they were told – no matter how small the offence – they had to be punished. Try to guess which crime earned which punishment…

CRIME	PUNISHMENT
I LAZINESS	A. DECIMATION OF A UNIT — I MAN IN EVERY X IS EXECUTED
II FALLING ASLEEP ON DUTY	B. SLEEP OUTSIDE THE SAFTEY OF THE CAMP
III RUNNING AWAY IN A BATTLE	C. GET THE WORST FOOD —ROUGH BARLEY INSTEAD OF GOOD CORN
IV PUTTING YOUR UNIT IN DANGER	D. DEATH BY BEATING
V RUNNING AWAY WITH YOUR UNIT	E. DEATH BY STONING

Answers

I B. II C. III D. IV E (Your unit would throw the stones). **V A** (The unlucky one in ten was chosen by drawing lots.)

Let the reward fit the action

Of course there were good sides to being a Roman soldier too – otherwise no one would have wanted to join the army! The goodies were...

I The army took two parts of every seven you earned in wages and saved it for you. When you retired they gave you all your savings and a piece of land. You could retire in comfort ... if you lived long enough.

2 You could make extra wealth by robbing the countries you defeated. You could take money, animals or even living prisoners that you could sell for slaves.

I THINK I'VE GOT THE SACK

3 For brave actions there were no medals – there were crowns:

a crown of oak leaves – for saving the life of a fellow citizen (Caesar won one at Mytilene when he was just 20 years old).

b a crown of plaited grass – for rescuing an army under siege.

c a crown of gold – for being the first soldier over the wall of an enemy town.

Don't get sick!

Roman doctors knew how to...

BUT – Roman doctors didn't know about anaesthetics (to put you to sleep while they hacked you about!).

Roman doctors could make medicines to cure sickness. BUT – they had to mix them with honey to try to disguise the disgusting tastes.

❝DID YOU KNOW? A ROMAN LEGIONARY ALWAYS WENT INTO BATTLE WITH A FIRST–AID KIT OF BANDAGES AND HEALING HERBS.❞

The Cut-Throat Celts

At one time the Celts had roamed round the world as much as the Romans did. One man put an end to all that – the Roman emperor, Julius Caesar.

The Celts used to fight fiercely for their tribal chiefs. But the tribes often fought against each other when they should have been fighting together against Julius Caesar. They needed one strong leader to bring them all together. But when that leader arrived it was too late.

WE'LL GET RID OF THE ROMANS AFTER WE'VE POLISHED OFF YOU!

YEAH!

OH YEAH?

Vercingetorix was a Celtic chief who was just as clever as Caesar at fighting and leading. Would you have been as clever as Vercingetorix? Here are some of the problems he faced. Could you have solved them?

Vercingetorix v Caesar

1 You meet the chiefs of the tribes every day to plan your war against Caesar. One of the chiefs argues against you. What do you do about him?

a Say to him, "Look, my friend, we must all stick together if we want to beat the rotten Romans. So, please, trust me. Remember, united we stand but divided we fall."

b Get upset. Say, "If you're going to argue with me you can find yourselves another leader. I'll fight Caesar by myself. When I've beaten him I'll beat you next. You'll be sorry!"

c Don't get upset. Simply have his ears cut off and one of his eyes gouged out. Send him back to his tribe with the message, "This is what you get if you mess with Vercingetorix!"

2 Caesar is a long way from home and a long way from fresh supplies. The Romans need food for the soldiers and their horses. They are getting it from the Celtic towns in the region of the Bituriges tribe. What can you do to stop them?

a Tell the Bituriges' chief to burn his towns to the ground and send his people to live with other tribes.

b Tell the Bituriges' chief to destroy all the food in the towns but let the people stay.

c Tell the Bituriges' chief to burn his towns to the ground but move all the people to the capital city of Avaricum.

3 Your tactics are working. Caesar is getting desperate for food. He sets off for Avaricum, which is the region's grain depot. How can you defend Avaricum against Caesar's army?

a Build a wooden wall.

b Build a stone wall with a ditch in front.

c Build a brick wall.

4 Caesar begins to build towers on wheels to push up to the walls. When these towers reach the walls the Romans will let down a drawbridge at the top and swarm over your walls. What can you do?

a Build an even taller tower behind your walls and throw down fireballs on top of them.

b Leave the town and attack. Caesar's towers.

c Run away.

A SIMPLE GUARD TOWER WOULD HAVE DONE

5 Caesar cannot get the towers near the walls because there is a ditch in front of the walls; He sends soldiers into the forest to chop down trees. He rolls the logs into the ditch and begins to fill it up. What can you do to stop the Romans filling the ditch?

a Dig a tunnel under your walls and set fire to the logs?

b Surrender.

c Send a raiding party out to steal the Roman axes so they can't chop down any more trees.

6 The Romans manage to get towers up to the walls. You would like to set fire to them but the clever Romans have covered them with leather, which doesn't catch fire very easily. What can you throw at them instead?

a Dead horses.

b Boiling fat and tar.

c Cold water.

7 Despite your efforts the Romans reach the walls. They catch hold of the top of the wall with hooks, and swarm up the ropes attached to the hooks. What's the best defence against this?

a Throw the hooks back.

b Pull the hooks up and drag them inside your fort.

c Wait for the Romans to climb them and try to kill them as they reach the top.

8 During the Roman assault it begins to rain heavily. What do your defenders do?

a Run for shelter until the rain stops and hope the Romans do the same.

b Fight on and get wet.

c Ask the Romans for a ceasefire until the weather improves.

9 The Romans reach the streets of Avaricum. They begin slaughtering every man, woman and child in sight. What should Vercingetorix do?

a Give himself up.

b Fight to the death.

c Make sure his best fighting men escape through a back entrance.

10 Vercingetorix reaches the safety of Alesia. The Romans are following. You have a large army. What should you do with it?

a Send most of the army away to gather help from other Celtic tribes and keep just a few to defend Alesia.

b Keep all the soldiers in Alesia and hope that help will arrive.

c Leave the army in Alesia and go for help yourself?

Vercingetorix's ten Steps to Rome, or, the answers:

1c Vercingetorix could not afford to show any weakness or he'd be killed by the other Celtic chiefs. He could not plead (**1a**) or sulk (**1b**). He had to show he meant business and would make an example of anyone who opposed him (**1c**).

2c Vercingetorix made just one mistake. He couldn't destroy the supplies and leave the people in the towns (**2b**) – the warriors would not have fought if they knew the Romans had captured their wives and children. He should have destroyed the supplies AND the towns (**2a**). If you chose **2a** then you'd have been a crueller but better leader than Vercingetorix! But the Bituriges were proud of Avaricum. They pleaded with Vercingetorix not to destroy it. He weakened and agreed (**2c**). From then on he was pretty well doomed.

3b Vercingetorix had fought the Romans for years and knew their way of fighting. They would have simply burned a wooden wall (**3a**) and battered down a brick wall (**3c**). The best wall was a solid stone wall with a ditch in front (**3b**).

4a Caesar wasn't put out by the solid walls of Avaricum. He began building towers. Vercingetorix expected this and didn't give up (**4c**). Of course, he didn't leave the safety of the town and attack the Romans in open battle (**4b**) because that's exactly what they wanted. He just ordered bigger towers to be built behind his own walls (**4a**).

5a Caesar could defeat the ditch by filling it with new logs. Vercingetorix couldn't stop him (**5c**) but didn't let it beat him (**5b**). The Bituriges were good iron miners and so could dig shafts. They dug one under the Roman logs and set fire to them (**5a**). This delayed the Roman attack … but failed to stop it.

6b The Celtic soldiers knew that the only thing that would slow down the Roman towers wasn't anything solid (**6a**), but liquid, which would run through the joins in the Roman "umbrella". Cold water wasn't going to hurt them (**6c**) but boiling tar and oil would. This is what they did (**6b**).

7b The Romans were determined – and getting hungrier! They began to use grappling hooks to climb the walls. There was no point in throwing them back (**7a**) because the Romans would just try again at another spot. No one had been able to stop the Romans by trying to kill them at the top (**7c**) because there were just too many of them. Clever Vercingetorix devised the plan of hauling up the hooks and taking away the Roman weapons (**7b**)!

8a When a rain-storm hit Avaricum, all of Vercingetorix's cleverness was undone by the stupidity of his men. They should have fought on (**8b**). The Romans wouldn't let some rain stop them (**8c**) and it was no use expecting them to. The defenders ran for shelter (**8a**). The Romans leapt over the walls.

9c Vercingetorix knew that the battle for Avaricum was lost, but the war wasn't. He wasn't going to give up (**9a**). On the other hand there was no point in waiting to be killed (**9b**) when there were new Celtic armies waiting to fight. All he had to do was to escape with the soldiers and fight again (**9c**). Unfortunately, the women who were being left behind to be massacred didn't like the idea. Not surprising really! They began wailing and screaming. This gave the escape plan away to the Romans and they hurried to cut off the escape route. The Romans massacred 40,000 Avaricum people. Only Vercingetorix and 800 others escaped to fight another day.

10a Vercingetorix reached the safety of Alesia with a new large army. If he'd tried to keep the army with him (**10b**) they'd have eaten the supplies in no time and starved to death before help arrived. He couldn't get to all the dozens of tribes himself to get help (**10c**) so he sent his troops to different Celtic tribes and kept just enough to defend the town (**10a**).

It almost worked. A huge Celtic army arrived. But the Romans had built a ring of defences round the town. The soldiers in Alesia couldn't get out. The new Celtic army couldn't get in. They gave up and went away.

Vercingetorix was trapped. He gave himself up to his own people and said they could do what they needed. The Romans wanted Vercingetorix alive – that was how the Celts delivered him. In 45 BC he was paraded through the streets of Rome ... then executed. The Celts on the continent were crushed. They survived mainly in the islands off the shores of Europe. The British Islands. If Caesar wanted to finish them off, then he had to invade Britain ... which he did.

That's why it's thought that the defeat of Vercingetorix led to the Roman invasion of Britain! If Vercingetorix had only destroyed Avaricum (as in **2a**) then we might never have had a Roman Britain!

Heads you win, heads you lose

Heads were popular with the Celtic race who were Rome's great enemy. Here are ten horrible brainless facts...

1 In 500 BC, the British tribes believed that the head had magical powers. They thought that severed heads could look into the future and give warnings, especially if they were in groups of three.

2 Rotting human heads were stuck on poles at the entrance to a hill fort.

3 Heads could be thrown into a lake or river as a gift to the gods.

4 After a battle the Celts rode from the battlefield with the heads of enemies dangling from the necks of their horses.

5 The heads might then be nailed to the walls of their houses.

6 Sometimes they were kept in cedar oil and taken out years later to show off to visitors. A Roman visitor said that the Britons would not part with their lucky heads for their weight in gold.

7 The Celtic Boii Tribe of the Po Valley (Northern Italy) took skulls and covered them in gold. They would then be used as cups!

8 Heads appeared in many ornaments of stone, metal or wood and paintings. Severed heads could be seen staring at you from the surface of tiles, pots, sword hilts, chariot fittings and even bucket handles!

9 Because the gods were more powerful than humans, they often had more heads. An Irish goddess, Ellen, had three heads! The druids had to keep her fed with sacrifices to stop her coming out of her underworld cave and ravaging the land.

10 The Britons even told stories about the magical power of the head. Many legends involved severed heads. One story is the Welsh legend of Bran the Blessed...

DAILY HEADLINE NEWS

HEADITOR : M.T. SKULL

BIG BRAN'S NOGGIN NICKED!

Some treacherous troublemaker has taken Britain's greatest treasure!

Yesterday the London burial place of Bran the Blessed was robbed. The great warrior's head was later found to be missing, along with another two skulls from the graveyard. The authorities are looking for a man with three heads!

Magical

As all our readers will know, the head of Bran the Blessed was the most magical article in the whole of Britain. Eight years ago Bran was mortally wounded in a bloody battle with an Irish king. As he lay dying he ordered the seven surviving soldiers to cut off his head and carry it with them. This they did and they found themselves in the afterlife as the guest of Bran – even though they weren't dead!

Then one warrior disobeyed one of Big Bran's orders. He opened a forbidden door. The warriors were heaved out of heaven. But, before they went, one of them tucked Brian's head up his tunic. And so it returned to earth. The head was buried in London, where it would guard Britain against evil for ever more.

Reward

Now it has been stolen there's no knowing what might happen. The *Daily Headline News* is offering a reward for information leading to its return.

Otherwise Britain will be heading for disaster!

Suffering slaves

"DID YOU KNOW?
THE ROMANS SOMETIMES TREATED SLAVES
BRUTALLY IN THEIR CONQUERED TERRITORIES
AND IN ROME ITSELF. IN AD 157 THE ROMAN
WRITER APULEIUS DESCRIBED LIFE IN A ROTTEN
ROMAN FLOUR MILL ... THE SLAVES WERE POOR,
SKINNY THINGS. THEIR SKIN WAS BLACK
AND BLUE WITH BRUISES,
THEIR BACKS WERE COVERED
WITH CUTS FROM THE WHIP.
THEY WORE RAGS, NOT CLOTHES,
AND HARDLY ENOUGH TO KEEP
THEM DECENT. THEY HAD A
BRAND MARK BURNED INTO THEIR
FOREHEAD AND HALF OF THEIR HAIR
WAS SHAVED OFF. THEY WORE CHAINS
AROUND THEIR ANKLES."

A slave revolt was led by Spartacus at a gladiator school near Naples. The slaves formed a huge army and terrorized the area for a couple of years. At last a Roman army defeated them. Over 6,000 slaves were crucified along the side of the main road from Capua to Rome.

Roman Revenge

One of the great heroes of the British tribes was Caratacus of the Catuvellauni tribe (north-west of London). While many tribal leaders were making peace with the Romans, Caratacus went on fighting. In the end he was defeated, of course. But he was still a hero.

That was one big difference. The Romans loved winners. The Britons seemed to love losers. The other difference was that the Romans learned from their mistakes. The Britons didn't.

It isn't likely that Caratacus could write. But, if he could, and if he kept a diary, would it have looked like this…?

Summer of AD 43 Kent

Disaster! I can't believe it! After two days of battle the Romans have defeated us. All we had to do was to stop them crossing the ~~Medway~~ River Medway. There's only one bridge over the Medway. All we had to do was sit tight on the northern end, wait for the Romans to cross it, then cut them into pieces…

... We'd have killed them in their thousands. We would! But what did they do??? They cheated!!! They sent troops upstream, they crossed where the water was shallow and attacked us from the back. That's not fair, is it?

Of course, we could have run them down with our chariots. We could! But what did they do? They cheated again!

They shot our horses. That's not fair, is it? They even killed my brother, Togodumnus. Poor, stupid Toggy. He should have done what I did. Retreated. Like dad always said, "He who fights and runs away, lives to fight another day."

So, I'm alive and next time I'll stuff those rotten Romans!!!!

Late Summer of AD43 - Dorset

Disaster! Again! The Romans are marching west. They're taking our hill-forts one after another. Of course, they don't fight fair. ~~It~~ They don't fight man to man ~~to~~ and let us kill them....

No. They shoot at our defenders with iron-tipped arrows. Hundreds at a time from some big machine. They drive us off the walls then swarm in after we've taken shelter.

They've taken 20 hill forts that way. I never thought I'd live to see the day they'd take the mighty Maiden Castle. In fact I nearly didn't live to see today! I just managed to retreat in time. He who fights and runs away.... But I'll stay in England. They'll never drive me into Wales.. Never!!

The other leaders are all surrendering, making peace and getting fat. But they won't get a hero like me. Not like they got poor old Toggy... ~~Net~~ Next time !!! I get them...

Summer of AD48 - Wales

Who is the greatest British leader ?? Caratacus. Me! Alright, so I'm stuck in the wild, wet Welsh mountains. But every now and then I lead a raid on some Roman troops and crack a few rotten Roman heads.

Actually it's rather hard to crack a Roman head. They wear these metal helmets. That's not fair, that's not. Some people might even call it cheating !

They'd like to drive me up to North Wales and into the Irish Sea. Well, there is absolutely NO chance of that. My men will fight to the death (Not my death of course. They need me alive to lead them)

I'll end up in North Wales over my warrior's dead bodies !!!

North Wales

Nth England

Welsh mountains

Dorset

Kent

North Wales - AD51

Disaster! Again!!! I never thought I'd see the day when the Romans would take a fort like Llanymynech. But they did. I still can't believe it. They couldn't attack Llanymynech from the back because that's a steep mountain face. They couldn't attack it from the front because that's the river Vyrnwy and the front wall of the fort.

But they did it! They crossed the river then came to the wall. We were pouring spears and stones and ~~and~~ arrows down on their heads. We should have massacred them...

So, what did they do? They cheated, ~~us~~ usual. They put their shields over their heads and came close together. The shields formed a solid wall over them. (They copied this from a Roman animal with a shell called a "tortoise" or something)

Our weapons just bounced off their "shell" and the Romans just kept coming till everyone was captured. The rotten Romans even took my family! I was lucky to escape. He who fights and runs away...... Still, next time I'll get them. I'm going to join forces with Queen Cartimandua of the Brigantes up near York ....

They're the biggest tribe outside of Roman rule. With me to lead them we'll chase the Romans all the way back to Rome. And they can take their tortoises with them.

I even hear old Claudius brought some huge grey monsters called elephants with him. They can take them back too!!! This time next year I'll be in Rome!!!

North England - later in AD 51

Life with Queen Cartimandua is great! I don't even miss my poor captured family. The beautiful Carti obviously fancies me. Can't blame her really. Me being the gretest British hero ever seen.

Loads of food. Better than living like an outlaw in the hills. And loads of wine. Lovely stuff. The very besht Roman wine. I wonder where she gets it from?

And she's even decorating me with chains. Chains on my wrists. Chains on my ankles. I fink that Carti loves me too show mush she wantsh to keep me here forever!!! I'm very shleepy now.

Nighty night Carti dear!

Next day

My head hurts. And worse. Much worse.
I'm a prisoner. I've found out where that
treacherous, ugly, vicious, lying Queen gets
her Roman wine from. She gets it from
the Romans!!! And what does she give
the Romans in return?

Me! I've been handed over to the Romans.
They're ~~that~~ taking me back to Rome. It's curtains
for Caratacus! I said I'd be in Rome within
a year, I never thought it would be in
chains. It's a disaster! They'll execute
me for sure. Me the greatest living British
hero. I'm not afraid to die of course... I just
don't want to be there when it happens.
' ' ' ' ' '

Next week -middle of the English Channel

I think I'm going to be sea-s...

Next month - Rome

What a place! These Romans really know how to treat a hero! Met old Claudius the emperor. Messy little weedy fellow. Dribbles and slobbers and limps about the place. But a very powerful man. Most important man in the world I reckon. And he spoke to me! (I didn't understand a word, of course, because he was blabbering away in Latin. But I could tell he <u>was</u> pleased to see me!)

Claudi gave an order and my chains were cut off. I thought, Aha! This is it! ~~this is~~ You're for the chop, Caratacus. But no! They treated me like a hero. They even said I was free to live in Rome. I think I might just do

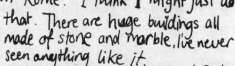

that. There are huge buildings all made of stone and marble. I've never seen anything like it.

Who wants to live in cold wet Britain in a draughty wooden hut? Not me! After all, I am the greatest British hero ever. I reckon I've earned an easy life with my old mate Claudi Maybe the rotten Romans aren't so rotten after all !!!

The diary might be made up, but the facts are about right. Caratacus arrived in Rome and told the Romans that they could only have great victories if they had great warriors (like himself) to fight against. "If you execute me, then all your glory will be forgotten," he warned them. Claudius agreed and released him.

But Caratacus was still puzzled when he saw the wealth of Rome. "When you Romans have all this, why do you want our poor huts?" Good question.

Meanwhile, back in Britain, the treacherous Cartimandua stayed in power (with Roman help) for another 15 years. Then her husband attacked her and kicked her out. The Romans really did take the British forts with ease. The Romans made mistakes. But they didn't usually make the same mistake twice. That's what made them so successful.

"DID YOU KNOW?
A MYSTERIOUS FUNERAL CEREMONY TOOK
PLACE NEAR LONDON IN THE
SECOND CENTURY AD.
A GRAVE HAS BEEN
DISCOVERED IN AN
UNDERGROUND ROOM BUT
IT CONTAINS NO HUMAN
BODIES. THERE ARE JUST
TWO CARVINGS OF MEN WHO
LOOK LIKE ROMAN SENATORS.
HISTORIANS THINK THAT THESE
MEN MUST HAVE DIED DURING
FIGHTING AND WERE BURIED
ELSEWHERE. IT SEEMS THAT THEY
DID NOT HAVE AN HONOURABLE
BURIAL ... MAYBE THEY WERE

TRAITORS. WHATEVER THE REASON THEIR CARVED HEADS WERE WALLED UP IN THIS ROOM TO BE FORGOTTEN. BUT ONE BODY WAS FOUND IN THE TOMB — THE BODY OF THE FAMILY CAT!"

Rotten Roman Leaders

Julius Caesar was one of the greatest Roman leaders. He was so great he was murdered ... by his friend! Rome had been run as a "republic" for many years. That is to say the important people in Rome decided what to do. Then Julius Caesar became so powerful there was a fear that he'd take over. The people thought he wanted to become "King of the Romans".

75

The last king they'd had was a disaster. His name was Tarquinius Superbus who lived in the 5th century BC. He took away certain rights of Romans and was the rottenest Roman of the time.

Was it true that Caesar wanted to be crowned king? And would he get to be as bad as Tarquinius? If so, it would be better to kill him now! This is how it happened...

Caesar's sticky end

1 Caesar had himself elected "Dictator for life" ... that was just another way of saying the dreaded word "King"!

2 Caesar started wearing red boots! Only a king wore red boots.

76

3 At a festival, Mark Antony, Caesar's friend, offered Caesar a diadem – a small crown. Caesar took it off – a sign that he didn't want to be king, perhaps? The crowds cheered when he took it off. But did Caesar and Mark Antony set this up to find out how the people felt? What if the people had cheered when the crown had been put on?

4 Caesar was due to speak to the Senate (the Roman parliament) on 15 March, 44 BC. Straight after his speech he was due to lead his troops into battle. During a war he'd be surrounded by his soldiers. No one could kill him then. If he was to die then he had to die on 15 March.

5 Caesar was a great believer in "fate" – if he was going to die then there was nothing he could do to change that. A fortune-teller told Caesar not to go to the Senate on 15 March. It didn't stop him.

6 Caesar's wife asked him not to go to the Senate that day. She'd had terrible nightmares and a feeling that something bad would happen. That didn't stop him.

7 Caesar felt ill on the morning of 15 March and was almost too ill to attend the Senate … he was worse by the time he left!

8 The killers chose Brutus as their leader. Brutus was one of the most popular men in Rome. He was famous for being honest. If he led the killing then the people of Rome would know the murderers were "honest" – that they did it for the good of the people.

9 On the evening of 14 March someone asked Caesar, "What sort of death would you like?" Caesar answered, "A sudden one." He got his wish.

10 Plutarch told the grim and gory story…

❝ When Caesar entered the Senate the senators all stood up as a sign of respect. Some of Brutus's gang slipped behind Caesar's chair while others came to meet him. Cimber grabbed Caesar's robe with both hands and pulled it from his neck. This was the signal for the attack…

Casca struck the first blow. His knife made a wound in Caesar's neck, but not a serious one, so that Caesar could still turn around, grab the knife, and hold on.

The watchers were horrified. They didn't dare run away or help Caesar or even make a sound.

Each assassin bared his dagger now. They all closed in on Caesar in a circle. They pushed him this way and that, like a wild beast surrounded by hunters. Brutus stabbed Caesar in the groin. Above all Caesar had trusted Brutus. Some say Caesar defended himself against all the rest – but when he saw Brutus coming at him with a dagger, he pulled his robe over his head and sank down.

*The attackers pushed Caesar
against the statue of his
old enemy, Pompey. The statue
became drenched with blood.
Caesar received 23 wounds.
Many of the assassins wounded each
other as they fought to stick so many
knives into one body.* 🙿

The killers made one big mistake. They didn't kill Mark Antony at the same time. "Honest" Brutus said it would be wrong. They were only out to stop wicked Caesar from becoming king. But it was Mark Antony who led a campaign of vengeance that destroyed the killers. Brutus committed suicide when he was defeated by Mark Antony at the battle of Philippi in 42 BC.

Caesar had left most of his fortune to his grandnephew, Octavian. Young Octavian became the sort of dictator that Caesar wanted to be. The thing the Romans feared – rule by one all-powerful man – had returned. And some of the emperors that followed were a hundred times worse than Julius Caesar!

In fact, some of the Roman Emperors were pretty weird. Here are the Rottenest Romans of all...

EMPEROR TIBERIUS
Ruled: AD 14–37

Favourite saying: "I don't care if they hate me … as long as they obey me!" (Know any teachers like that?)

Nastiest habit:
Breaking the legs of anyone who disobeyed him.

Rottenest act: Tiberius needed a holiday. "I think I'll take a break!" he announced. As the servants scuttled off to find their shinpads he cried, "A holiday, I mean. A short break on the island of Capri off the south coast of Italy would be very nice."

83

He had only been there a few days when a humble Capri fisherman caught a large crab and a huge mullet fish. The poor man decided that it would make a wonderful gift for the visiting emperor. The cliff was steep and there was no track. The mullet was heavy. The fisherman struggled for an hour and finally reached the top.

"Take me to the emperor," he pleaded with the guard.

"The emperor wishes to be left alone today," the guard said, shaking his head.

"It's the biggest mullet I've ever caught!" the fisherman said proudly. "The gods meant it for the emperor. Tell the emperor I must see him!"

84

The guard shrugged. It was a boring life, standing on the top of the cliff watching the gulls. The emperor might order him to break the fisherman's legs. "I'll see what the emperor says," he smirked.

Five minutes later he returned and said with a grin. "The emperor will see you now."

The poor little man dragged the huge fish into the emperor's room. "You'll be sorry," the guard muttered.

As the fisherman stepped through the door two huge guards grabbed his arms. "I've brought a gift for the emperor!" he squeaked.

Tiberius stepped forward. "You disturbed my rest you smelly little man!" he snarled.

"It's the fish, your worship!" the fisherman cried.

"No!" the emperor jeered. "That fish smells sweeter than you. Guards!"

"Sir?"

"Sweeten the little man. Rub that fish over his body!"

"It was a present ... ouch! Mullet scales are very rough!" he screamed.

The guard scrubbed the rough skin over the fisherman's face till the skin was scraped off and his face left raw and bleeding. The guard smiled as he stripped the skin off the fisherman's chest.

"Ahh! Oooh!" the man wailed.

"Enough!" the emperor snapped. The guards let the fisherman fall to the floor where he lay groaning and muttering something through his bleeding lips.

"What did you say?" Tiberius growled.

"I just said thank the gods I didn't bring you that big crab I caught this morning," the little man burbled.

The emperor's eyes lit up with evil glee. "Go to this man's house and fetch the crab," he chuckled.

The guard nodded. As he left the emperor's room he winked at the sobbing fisherman. "I told you that you'd be sorry."

And after being scrubbed with the sharp shell of a crab the little man was so sorry that he wished he'd never been born.

Sticky end: Tiberius died at the age of 77, probably suffocated by his chief helper. The Roman people went wild with joy!

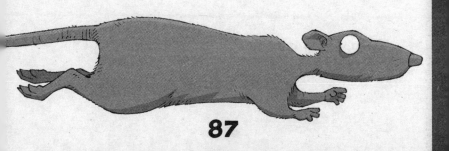

CALIGULA
Ruled: AD 37–41

Favourite sayings:
To his friends at a banquet, "It has just occurred to me that I only have to give one nod and your throats will be cut."

To the guards of a row of criminals, "Kill every man between that one with the bald head and that one over there."

To his people, "Rome is a city of necks just waiting for me to chop."

To everyone who would listen, "I am a god."

Nastiest habit: "His little jokes". At a sacrifice ceremony he was given a hammer which would knock out the beast to be sacrificed. The priest was waiting to cut the beast's throat. Caligula hit the priest over the head instead!

Rottenest act: Caligula loved to organize huge killing festivals with loads of spectators. There were fights to the death between gladiators, and fights with wild animals. But the wild animals had to be kept alive until the day of the contest. Caligula was shocked at the cost of the raw meat needed to feed the animals. So he found a cheap supply of meat ... he fed criminals to them!

Daftest act: He tried to make his dear friend Incitatus a consul – so Incitatus almost became one of the most powerful rulers in the Roman Empire. So? So, Incitatus was his favourite horse!

Sticky end: One of his trusted guards stabbed him to death. Others went to the palace where they killed his wife and child.

CLAUDIUS
Ruled: AD **41–54**

Favourite saying: "Kk-k-k-k-k- … er … execute him!"

Nastiest habit: Watching criminals being tortured and men being executed by being flogged to death.

Rottenest act: Claudius discovered his wife was a bit of a flirt and had wild parties with her friends. Claudius not only had her executed but 300 party friends went too.

Sticky end: His niece, Agrippina, poisoned him with mushrooms.

NERO
Ruled: AD 54–68

Favourite sayings: He played the lyre very badly but people told him he was brilliant. The Greeks were particularly creepy about telling him he was good. "Only the Greeks are worth my genius," he would say.

When he knew he had to die all he could say was, "What a loss I shall be to the art of music!"

Nastiest habit: Murdering people. He had his half-brother, Britannicus, poisoned. Actually, Britannicus had a food taster who ate and drank a tiny bit of every dish that the Emperor was going to eat. If the food was poisoned, the taster would die first. The taster drank some hot wine and passed it over to the emperor. The taster was fine. The wine was "safe" to drink. But Britannicus complained that the wine was too hot and ordered water to cool it. Then he drank it ... and died. The cold water had been poisoned!

Nero had his first wife, Octavia, murdered. Her head was sent to Nero's new girlfriend, Poppaea. But then he murdered Poppaea, too.

Nero had Christians persecuted
cruelly...

• They would be
tied to a post,
covered in tar and
set alight.

• They would be
covered in animal
skins and thrown to
hungry, wild dogs.

• They were crucified
in large numbers.

Rottenest act: Agrippina had poisoned Claudius
and now her son, Nero, was emperor. She thought
she could rule the empire through her weak and
wicked son.

Nero had other ideas. His mother was always interfering – stopping his meeting with his girlfriend, Acte, because she wasn't royal. Agrippina had to go.

First Nero made up with Agrippina after their row over Acte. Then he invited mum to join him at a party on the Bay of Naples. Agrippina was happy to accept, glad to be  friends with her son once more.

Nero sent a boat to pick her up. A special boat with special oarsmen. For the boat was designed to fall apart at sea and the oarsmen were instructed not to let Agrippina return alive. The boat set off on a beautiful starry night.

But the boat didn't fall apart. There were heavy weights on the wooden canopy over Agrippina's seat. At the right moment they were to crash through the canopy, kill Agrippina and fall through the bottom of the boat to sink it. Everyone would say the boat hit a rock. Sad accident. Poor Nero, losing his loving mother.

That's what was meant to happen. But, when the weights fell through the roof they killed Agrippina's friend. Agrippina and her other friend, Aceronnia escaped ... and the boat didn't sink!

The oarsmen tried to rock the boat to capsize it. That's when Aceronnia did a very brave thing. She began to cry out, "Save me! I am Agrippina, the emperor's mother! I am Agrippina!"

And in the darkness the oarsmen believed her. They battered her to death with their oars while the real Agrippina slipped over the side and escaped back to her palace. She sent a message to Nero saying what a lucky escape she'd had.

Nero was furious. He decided to make sure the next time. He sent two murderers to her palace. Agrippina thought they'd come from Nero to find out if she was all right!

As the first one battered her with a club she realized her mistake. When the other drew his sword she bared her stomach and invited him to stab her where the ungrateful Nero had come from. He did.

Nero reported that she had killed herself!

Sticky end: When he knew that the Roman Army had deserted him and rebels were coming to arrest him, he placed a sword to his throat. One of his friends gave him a push. The arresting officer arrived as he bled to death.

Ten funny facts about Roman emperors

1 Emperor Caligula's real name was Gaius. Caligula was just a nickname meaning "little boot". This was because he liked dressing up and playing at being a soldier from a very early age.

2 Caligula wanted to copy Julius Caesar and invade Britain. In AD 40 he went to the Roman base in Boulogne (in northern France) where he set sail to lead the invasion. He turned back when he saw that no one wanted to follow him!

3 Augustus Caesar was one of the kinder emperors. But even he had his moments – the murder of Julius Caesar really upset him. As Suetonius said, "Augustus showed no mercy to his beaten enemies.

He sent Brutus's head to Rome to be thrown at the feet of Caesar's statue."

4 Julius Caesar gave us our modern calendar. The early Romans had 12 months plus a 13th month that was added every four years. In 46 BC Caesar gave us the 12-month, 365-day year with the 29-day February leap year.

5 Emperor Heliogabalus enjoyed the hobby of collecting cobwebs ... by the ton!

6 Honorius loved chickens. His favourite chicken was called Rome. He was hiding in his country mansion, safe from the invading army of Goths. When the city of Rome was overrun by Alaric and his army of Goths, a messenger arrived to say, "Rome is lost!" Honorius was heart-broken...

"ROME IS LOST"

EEK!

...until someone told him the messenger meant the capital city and not the hen.

7 Nero enjoyed the cruel "circuses" so much that he had to take part. He was dressed in the skins of wild animals and locked in a cage. The human victims were tied to stakes in the arena. Nero's cage was opened. He leapt out and attacked the victims.

8 When Emperor Pertinax was murdered there wasn't just one person to take his place. Two men claimed the throne. Both men thought it would be useful to have the support of the emperor's praetorian guard – so they tried to outbid each other for it. Julianus won. He made an offer of 25,000 sesterces (Roman money) to each man. Unfortunately he couldn't afford to pay all the men in all the Roman armies across the world. They attacked and threw him out after just 66 days on the throne. The money he spent on bribing the emperor's guards was wasted – they were easily tricked into giving up their weapons.

9 In the 50 years between AD 235 and AD 285 there were about 20 emperors. Most of them were there a short time, murdered and replaced by the murderer who was murdered and replaced by the murderer, and so on. Some of the senior Romans refused to become emperor at this time – not surprising really!

10 Septimius had particularly nasty family problems. He had two sons, Caracalla and Geta. Caracalla was allowed to become joint emperor when he was just 13. Caracalla had his father-in-law murdered, then set off with his father and brother to conquer Scotland. During the campaign,

Caracalla threatened to kill his father – but didn't. Old Septimius died in York and his dying words to his sons were, "Do not disagree with each other." Fat chance. Within a year Caracalla had brother Geta murdered. Caracalla was sole emperor at last. He kept the throne for five years, then ... no prizes for guessing what happened to him.

Yes, he was murdered.

**❝DID YOU KNOW?
JULIUS CAESAR
PASSED BURIAL LAWS
FOR THE PEOPLE WHO LIVED
IN THE NEW TOWNS BUILT
IN THE ROMAN EMPIRE,**

THESE WERE...

"No one may bring, burn or bury a dead person within the boundaries of the town."

"No crematorium shall be built within half a mile of a town."

(BURIAL SITES HAD TO BE EITHER OUTSIDE THE CITY WALLS OR JUST INSIDE. CAESAR WANTED A PERFECT TOWN FULL OF GRAND BUILDINGS AND FRESH AIR FOR HIS FAITHFUL FOLLOWERS.)**"**

Rotten Roman Childhood

Children had a tough time in the age of the rotten Romans from the moment they were born. One writer, Soranus, described how each new-born child was laid on the earth and allowed to cry for a while before it was washed and clothed. Only the fit survived.

Some of the Germans in the Roman Empire gave their new-born children an even worse test. They dunked the child in cold water. If the baby came out purple with the cold or shivering then it was a weakling – it wasn't worth bringing up so it was left to die!

Girls were named eight days after they were born – boys on the ninth day. Girls would usually take their father's name – but change the "-us" on the end to "-a".

So the daughter of Julius became Julia, the daughter of Claudius was Claudia, Flavius was the father of Flavia and so on.

Children would probably have "pet names" or nicknames. One girl was known as "Trifosa" – that means "delicious"!

The Celt names had their own meanings...

- Boudicca meant "Victory"
- Cartimandua meant "White Filly"
- Grata meant "Welcome"

Then, if you survived your birth, and you could live with your name, you had to face the terrors of the rotten Roman schools...

Suffering schoolchildren – the good, the bad and the awful

Good: Schools cost parents money, so only the parents who could afford it sent their children. If you were poor you could miss going to school altogether.

Bad: Slave children didn't go to school. They were born slaves and belonged to the master.

Awful: Poor children missed school but had to work twice as hard for parents. If you didn't your parents might just decide to sell you! It was illegal to sell free children as slaves – but this didn't stop poor parents from doing it. There was not much chance of their being caught.

Good: Education was divided rather as it is today into primary, secondary and college.

Bad: Most children only went as far as primary.

Awful: For laziness in primary school you'd get the cane or a beating if the teacher didn't have a cane handy. One poet described his bullying teacher like this...

His mouth's no good – but he has a hard fist. Why doesn't he become a boxer instead?

WHO ELSE FORGOT TO DO THEIR HOMEWORK?

Good: Primary schools usually had just 10 to 12 children.

Bad: That was not enough to pay a teacher's wage. So the poor teacher had another job – maybe in a workshop.

Awful: The Romans didn't have the figure zero. That made sums rottenly difficult to teach. Ask your teacher, "Can you add LXXXVIII and XII?" (The answer is "C".)

Good: At least schoolchildren had their own goddess. Her name was Minerva. The holiday for the goddess was in March. After the holiday the school year began.

Bad: Each child had to provide their own wax tablets and stylus (sharp pen to scratch letters into the wax), their pen and ink, their paper rolls and abacus (counting frame).

Awful: For a serious offence in the secondary school – a flogging with a leather whip while other pupils held you down.

Good: Schools closed every ninth day for the market – it was probably too noisy to teach on market days.

Bad: Primary schools were pretty boring. You'd study mainly the three "Rs"– reading, 'riting and 'rithmetic.

114

Awful: At secondary school you had to study mega-boring grammar and literature, with some geography and, of course, horrible history! By the time you got to college you had to study for public speaking – the Romans believed that good talkers made good leaders. (Do you agree?)

WHO WROTE THAT!

HISTORY HORRIBILIS

A grim life for girls

Through most periods of history it's been harder being a woman than being a man. It was no different in Roman Britain...

1 Roman girls were lucky … if they lived!

"If you give birth to a boy, look after it – but if it is a girl then let it die!"

   (*Letter from Hilarion to his wife.*)

2 Men weren't happy with the idea of an educated woman. "I hate a woman who reads", wrote Juvenal in the 1st century AD.

3 Roman women had to be "controlled" from an early age. They were given a lucky charm at birth. Why? Because they didn't have a man of their own to protect them. When a baby girl was eight days old she was taken to a special ceremony. A gold or leather heart was hung around her neck. She would keep it throughout her childhood.

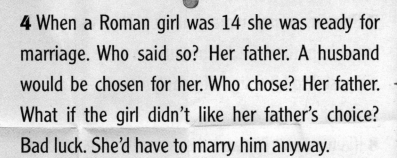

4 When a Roman girl was 14 she was ready for marriage. Who said so? Her father. A husband would be chosen for her. Who chose? Her father. What if the girl didn't like her father's choice? Bad luck. She'd have to marry him anyway.

5 On the evening before the wedding a special event took place. The girl placed all her toys and childhood clothes on the altar of the Lares – the household gods. She also took off her lucky charm – she had a husband to protect her now.

6 The bride always wore a white woollen tunic. It was held at the waist with a woollen belt tied in a special knot. She wore a bright yellow cloak and sandals. Her head was covered with a flame-coloured veil.

7 Roman women wore make-up. They used chalk to whiten their necks because a pale skin was supposed to be a sign of beauty.

8 If a woman's lips and cheeks weren't red enough then they would use a reddish earth called ochre.

9 Women were expected to remove hair from their legs as well as from under their arms. They rubbed hair off with a stone or used a cream to dissolve it and it's a wonder the creams didn't dissolve the skin too! One hair-remover consisted of the blood of a wild she-goat mixed with sea-palm and powdered viper. Then, if you wanted to stop the hair growing back again, you would have to rub on the blood of a hare.

10 If a girl's eyebrows weren't dark enough then she might have used metallic stuff called antimony. No antimony? Then girls used ashes! Imagine walking around with mud on your face, chalk on your neck and ashes on your eyebrows. If you got carried away you'd look more like a scarecrow.

Rotten Roman stories

The Romans knew some pretty rotten stories. Stories of gods, graves and guts. Their own gods were a bit boring. But then they heard the stories of the Greek gods. Those gods were much more like interesting people. So the Romans pinched the Greek legends and made them their own. Stories like that of Prometheus…

The Eagle has landed … again … and again … and again…

The fat, feathered fiend landed on the rock and looked at the man who lay chained to it. The bird's beak was as hooked as a hairpin. His great golden eyes glinted in the harsh sun. "Cor! Stone the crows! What a tasty sight!" he croaked. If he'd had lips he would have licked them.

Instead he licked his beak.

The young prisoner lifted his head wearily. He was a handsome young man with nothing on but a loin cloth. He squinted through the fierce sun and glared at the bird. "Push off," he snapped.

The bird hopped from one hot foot to the other. Hey! That's no way to speak to me! I'll have you know I'm an eagle – king of the birds!"

"Sorry, I'm sure," the man sneered. "I should have said, 'push off, your highness'."

The eagle shrugged. "No need to be offensive. I'm only doing my job. And a bird's gotta do what a bird's gotta do!"

"And I'm tired of every sparrow on Mount Olympus stopping off here to gawp and stare," the prisoner spat.

The bird breathed in deeply and ruffled its

breast feathers importantly. "I am here on a mission. Some old geezer at the top of the mountain sent me."

"The gods live at the top of the mountain," the man said.

"Yeah, well some old god sent me, then. Big guy with long white hair and a bushy great beard."

"Zeus!"

"Bless you ... anyway, he said, 'Fly down there and you'll see young Prometheus chained to a rock,'" the eagle went on.

"That's me! You've brought me the news that the great god Zeus has forgiven me? I'm to be set free?"

"Nah! The old guy told me to fly down here, and eat your liver."

"Eat my liver?" the young god groaned.

"Well, I didn't argue, did I?" the eagle chuckled. "I like a nice bit of fresh liver. Specially when it's fried with a few onions."

"You'll kill me!" Prometheus cried.

"Nah! You're immortal. You'll 'liver' long time yet! Heh! Heh! Heh!" the bird cackled.

The god blinked as sweat ran into his eyes.

123

"You'll hurt me," he sniffed.

"Can't be helped," the bird croaked and took a step towards his victim. "You must have done something pretty bad to deserve this!"

Prometheus sighed and looked towards the sun. "Once I could move through the air, just like you. One day I flew up to the sun itself. I brought its fire back down to earth."

"Good thing too – otherwise I'd have to eat your liver raw," the eagle chuckled nastily.

The young god went on, "I gave it to the humans to use."

"Sounds fair enough to me," the eagle admitted.

"Ah, but Zeus had told me not to give fire to the humans. He was furious. My punishment is to be chained to this mountainside."

"And to have your liver eaten," the eagle

reminded him.

"Must you?" Prometheus groaned.

"Cor, stone the crows. You're supposed to be a hero, ain't you? Well, stop whingeing and let me get me dinner."

The bird lunged forward and Prometheus screamed.

When it was over the bird gripped the dripping liver in its talons and opened its wings. The mountain air lifted it gently off the mountainside and the eagle soared upwards. "See you tomorrow, Prommy!" it cried.

"Tomorrow!" Prometheus screamed. "What bit of me are you going to eat tomorrow?"

"Same again!" the eagle cawed. "That's the worst bit of the punishment. Your liver grows back. I'll come back tomorrow and eat it again ... and the next day … and the next … until the end of time! Bye for now!"

Prometheus twisted his head to look at his side. There wasn't a mark to show the eagle's work.

And every day the eagle returned. Day after day, month after month and year after year. Until one day…

"Hello there, Prom!" the eagle called happily as it clattered down on to the sun-warmed rock.

"Hello, Eddie," Prometheus grinned.

The eagle took a step back. "Er … you look happy this morning, Prom!"

The young god nodded happily. There was a gleam of pure nastiness in his eyes. Suddenly his hand shot forward and he grabbed the bird around its thick neck.

"Awk!" it squawked. "Your chains!"

"A friend of mine came along and snapped them for me," Prometheus smiled and his grip on the eagle's neck tightened. A huge man stepped from behind the rock. He had muscles that rippled like waves on the sea. "Meet Hercules. The greatest hero ever to walk the earth."

"Pleased to meet you, Herc!" the eagle

OOPS

gasped. "Er … if you'll just let me go, Prom, I'll get off back to me nest."

"You're going nowhere," Prometheus promised.

"Nah! I was getting sick of liver anyway," the big bird said weakly.

"Hercules is going to kill you," Prometheus said calmly.

"Look Prommy … mate … old pal … there was never anything personal, you know! I was only doing my job! Stone the crows, a bird's gotta do what a bird's gotta—"

His words were choked off with Prometheus's tight hand. He ignored the eagle's words. "But before I let Hercules kill you, guess what I'm going to do?"

"Er … me liver?" the bird guessed.

Prometheus nodded.

"Aw, no, Prommy. It'll taste really nasty – yeuch! Honest! Really sour."

"Ah, but you're forgetting one thing, Eddie. There's nothing in this world that tastes so sweet as … revenge!"

"DID YOU KNOW?
THE FOUNDERS OF ROME, ROMULUS
AND REMUS, WERE SUPPOSED TO
HAVE SURVIVED BEING LEFT TO DIE
ON A HILLSIDE. A SHE-
WOLF ADOPTED THEM.
WHEN THEY GREW UP,
ROMULUS KILLED
REMUS AND CREATED
ROME – NAMED AFTER
ROMULUS, OF COURSE. IF HE
HADN'T, THEN THIS BOOK
MIGHT HAVE BEEN CALLED,
THE ROTTEN REMANS!"

Rotten Roman Fun and Games

Rotten Roman games

Which of the following modern games do you think the Romans had?

① HIDE-AND-SEEK

② TAG

③ COMPUTER GAMES

④ HOPSCOTCH

⑤ DOLLS WITH MOVING ARMS AND LEGS

⑥ LEAPFROG

⑦ KITES

⑧ BUILDING BLOCKS

⑨ SEE SAW

⑩ SWING

131

Some Roman games you might like to try

Roman children's games were a bit like ours ... only rottenly vicious at times!

Trigon

• Next time your parents slaughter a pig for dinner, ask them for the bladder – it's a part you won't be eating anyway.

• The bladder is cleaned out, then blown up like a balloon and tied.

THPURP

OOPS

TIED TIGHT

• A triangle with sides about two metres long is drawn on the ground and a player stands at each corner of the triangle.

• The bladder-ball is passed from one player to another without it touching the ground.

• The aim of the game is to keep the bladder-ball in the air as long as possible.

• Easy? Then add two more balls so that each player has one. There is no set order for passing the ball. You may have to pass your ball while receiving two from the other players! (Game hint: It helps to have three hands.)

• If you drop a ball you lose a point. The winner is the one with the fewest drops in the time – say five minutes. (If you can't find a dead pig then use tennis balls.)

Knucklebones

- If your parents happen to sacrifice a sheep to the gods, ask if you can have one of its feet.
- Boil the sheep's foot until the flesh and skin fall away from the bones.
- Take the small, cubic bones and dry them. You now have five "chuck stones".
- Hold the bones in one hand. Throw them into the air. The aim is to see who can catch the most on the back of the hand.

(Note: If your parents aren't sacrificing any sheep this week, you can use stones, dice or cubes of wood.)

GULP!

134

Micare

- Play in pairs.
- Each player places their right hand behind their back.
- Agree on a signal – one player will nod, for example.
- On the signal, both players shoot out the right hand with a number of fingers raised.
- At the same moment each player calls out what they guess the total number of fingers will be.
- If neither guesses correctly then try again.
- The winner is the first one to guess correctly. (Note: This sounds easy. In fact, the more you play it, the more you learn to use clever tactics. Try it and see.)

The Jar Game

- Someone is selected to be "It".

- "It" sits on the ground – they are said to be "in the jar". The others try to prod or nip the one on the ground – rotten Roman children could be pretty vicious while playing this. (Warning! Only pinch or punch "It" if "It" happens to be a teacher).

- The person in the jar cannot get up but they can try to grab hold of one of the touchers.

- The toucher who is grabbed goes into the jar.

Nuts

• Each player has a supply of nuts – probably hazelnuts.

• Each player adds a nut to her/his pile to build a pyramid.

• The winner is the player who uses the most nuts before the pyramid collapses.

(Note: This is a game for children. When you grew up the Romans would say you had "left your nuts". Perhaps you would like to ask your teacher, "When did you leave your nuts?")

Blind Man's Buff

• Someone is chosen to be blindfolded.

• The other players each have a stick and dance around tapping the "blind man" with the stick, shouting "Come and catch me!", which the blindfolded person tries to do.

• If a player is caught then the blindfolded person tries to guess who s/he is holding.

• If the blindfolded person is right then the caught player becomes the blindfolded one.

FUNNY... IT'S ALL GONE QUIET

Word games

If you like word games or crosswords then you might like to make a "square" of words. They should read the same whether they are read from left to right or from top to bottom.

Here's an example from Reading in Roman Britain (now in Berkshire) It was found scratched on a tile...

Sator means "a sower".

Arepo is a man's name.

Tenet means "he holds".

Opera means "work" or "deeds".

Rotas means "wheels".

The square has also been translated as "The sower, Arepo, guides the wheels carefully."

BUT … some clever person worked out that this was not a word game at all, but a secret, Christian prayer! Take all the letters and you can spell out the word PATERNOSTER. This is Latin for "Our Father" – the opening of the Lord's Prayer. There are two "A"s and two "O"s left over. These letters represent "the beginning and the end" to early Christians.

Clever, yes? But is it just coincidence? Or is it really a prayer? Make up your own mind.

140

Rotten grown-up games

The Romans enjoyed their circuses. But they weren't the sort of family day out we have at the circus today. No clowns, no jugglers, no tightrope walkers. But lots of violence, blood and death.

Augustine of Hippo wrote a book in which he told of his disgust at the bloodshed. His friend, Alypius, was taken to a Roman circus by some student friends. He set off for the circus, a real wimp. A band of trumpets played, bets were placed and the fighting began…

141

He shut his eyes tightly, determined to have nothing to do with these horrors. If only he had closed his ears as well! The fight drew a great roar from the crowd! This thrilled him so deeply that he could not contain his curiosity. When he saw the blood it was as though he had drunk a deep cup of savage passion. Instead of turning away he fixed his eyes upon the scene and drank in all its frenzy. He revelled in the wickedness of the fighting and was drunk with the fascination of the bloodshed.

Julius Caesar, on the other hand, became a bit bored with the fighting and the dying. Long before the end of a contest he would begin reading reports and writing letters. This did not make him very popular with some of the spectators in the crowds!

Gruesome gladiators – ten terrible truths

1 The Romans brought the gladiator fights to Britain ... battles between teams of armed men of whom half would be sure to lose their lives.

2 The idea of fighting and killing as a game probably began at funerals. The Roman Tertullian said...

Once upon a time, people believed that the souls of the dead were kept happy with human blood, and so, at funerals, they sacrificed prisoners of poor quality

DO I GET A SACRIFICE AT MY FUNERAL?

These sacrifices changed into fights to the death between two men at the funeral. They became so popular that they were taken away from the funeral and put in a huge arena. The fighters became known as gladiators.

3 In Rome there had been schools of gladiators, where a slave could train and fight for a gladiator master. If he won enough battles – and murdered enough opponents – he would win a fortune and his freedom. The greatest prize was the wooden sword a symbol of freedom.

4 Nutty Nero even ordered a battle between a woman and a dwarf as a special spectacle.

5 When a victim fell in a fight an attendant would smack him on the head with a hammer to make sure he was dead.

6 If a fighter gave up, exhausted, he could surrender. The emperor would then decide if he deserved to live or not. The crowd would usually tell him by screaming, "Mitte! Let him go!" or "Iugula! Kill him!" The emperor would signal his decision with his thumb. Thumb down for death – thumb up for life. And we still use that sign today.

7 Some of the bloodiest battles were between criminals who were under sentence of death anyway. They fought till there was no one left – an unarmed man was put in the ring with an armed man who killed him. The armed man was then disarmed and the next man killed him. And so it went on – as soon as one victim fell, another was put in the ring.

8 There's not much evidence to show that the Romans in Britain brought the sort of wild animals to the arena that they brought to Rome itself.

9 There would be bears from Scotland, which were chained to a post and tormented for the entertainment of the crowd.

10 Back in Rome they would have seen…

• elephants fight against armed men – until one day, the elephants crashed through iron railings and trampled the crowd. Caesar had a moat built round the arena to protect the spectators from the animals.

• sea battles in an arena which could be flooded to take warships.

• animals fighting each other to the death – bear against buffalo, buffalo against elephant, elephant against rhinoceros.

• crocodiles, giraffes, hippopotami and ostriches – the crocodiles were tricky because they didn't survive very well when taken out of Africa. One lot spoiled the fun by refusing to eat!

SLAVES SLAVES SLAVES, WHERE'S THE VARIETY?

• men against panthers, lions, leopards, tigers – but the men were usually heavily armed with spears, flaming torches, bows, lances and daggers. Some even took a pack of hounds into the arena to help them – they were in no more danger than the audience! One spectator made a joke about the emperor, Domitian. He was taken out of the crowd and thrown to a pack of dogs!

• men with cloaks against bulls – of the kind you can still see in Spain today.

• men fighting bears with their bare fists.

• five thousand beasts killed in one day of AD 80 in the Colosseum of Rome.

Amazing acts

But not every show in the arena was violent. Some of the acts used tame animals to perform tricks, rather as circus animals do today. The spectators were amused by...

- teams of tame panthers pulling chariots.
- a lion releasing a live hare from its mouth after it had caught it.
- a tiger licking the hand of its trainer.
- elephants kneeling in the sand in front of the emperor.
- elephants tracing Latin words in the sand with their trunks.

Petrifying plays

The Romans liked to visit the open-air theatres to watch plays. There were theatres in many of the bigger British towns. But if the plays were anything like the plays back in Rome, they would be banned today for being too violent!

The actors had real fights on stage. Then, Emperor Domitian allowed a real death on the stage. At the end of the play "Laureolis" the villain has to be crucified, tortured and torn apart by a bear. The actor playing the villain left the stage and his place was taken by a criminal who was under the sentence of death. The really rotten Romans enjoyed watching this horrible spectacle.

Then, of course, the Romans used the arenas as an excuse to execute people they didn't like – they put men, women and children in with wild animals, sometimes just for the simple crime of being Christians.

Strangely, it was the Christian religion that finally put an end to the massacres. When the emperors became Christian they banned the bloodthirsty events. On 1 October AD 326, Emperor Constantine put a stop to the gladiator schools and, by the end of the century, the shows had disappeared from the empire.

"DID YOU KNOW?
THE TERM ROMAN HOLIDAY IS STILL
USED TO DESCRIBE PEOPLE ENJOYING
THEMSELVES BY WATCHING OTHERS
SUFFERING. SO, WHEN TEACHERS TRY TO
TELL YOU THE ROMANS
"CIVILIZED" THE
BARBARIANS, YOU CAN
TELL THEM THAT THE ROTTEN
ROMANS HAD SOME OF THE
MOST "UNCIVILIZED" FUN
AND GAMES IN HISTORY."

Rotten Roman Food

The richest Romans enjoyed tasty foods and new recipes. They could afford spices to disguise the boring taste of the smoked or salted meat and fish.

Twenty foul food facts

1 The rich had great feasts. One Roman, called Trimalchio, held a feast which included wine that was a hundred years old. It also included a wild boar that, when sliced down the belly, allowed song-thrushes to fly out.

2 During such feasts some guests could eat so much that they had to be sick. They would then go back into the dining room to continue eating!

3 Emperor Maximian was a big eater. He was supposed to have eaten 20 kilograms of meat a day … that's about all the meat you'd get from a small sheep!

4 Maximian's enemies said he drank 18 bottles of wine with each meal. Such gluttony killed him in the end, of course … but not until he'd reigned almost 20 years!

5 In the kitchen, the rich kept a special container used for fattening up their dormice. They were fed on the very best food – walnuts, acorns and chestnuts, before being killed, stuffed and served as a great delicacy. The stuffing could be made from pork sausage (or even sausage made from other dormice) and flavoured with pepper and nuts.

6 Snails fattened in milk were popular. Take your live snails out of their shells and put them in a shallow dish of milk and salt for a day. They love milk so they slurp it down, but the salt just makes the stupid creatures thirstier! Then they are placed in plain milk for a few days. They drink and drink till they become too fat to get back in their shells. Fried in oil and served covered in wine sauce – they are delicious!

7 Even fouler ... fatten up the snails on blood to add to their flavour. (Some snails would be vampire snails given the chance!)

8 The Romans enjoyed stuffed thrush. No worse than your Sunday chicken, right? Wrong! They stuffed the thrush through the throat without taking the insides out! Yeuch! The Romans also ate other birds that we wouldn't usually think of eating. They enjoyed...

- herring-gulls
- jackdaws
- peacocks
- ravens
- swans
- crows
- coots

9 The Romans didn't waste much. One recipe by Apicius calls for the chopped-up udder of a sow. They also ate the brains of animals ... not to mention the lungs of goats and sheep.

10 King Mithradates of Pontus in Asia was scared of being poisoned, so he ate … poison! In small doses, of course. That way his body built up a resistance to poison. Then he heard the Romans were coming to get him and he hadn't the guts to face them. So he swallowed poison. Of course, it didn't work! He had to fall on his sword in the end. (So, when the Romans found him he had even less guts!)

This just isn't my day.

11 The Romans had some rotten sauces too. One was made from the guts of fish. They were salted and left to rot in the sun. After a few days the liquid was drained off and drunk or used as a sauce – the way you may sprinkle tomato ketchup on your chips. (This may sound a fishy story, but it's true!)

12 The Romans ate chicken, duck and goose, just as we still do. But the Romans probably served them at the table with the heads cut off but the feet still on!

13 In Roman times there were storks living in Britain. The Romans ate those too.

14 Horse bones have been found at Verulamium, which shows that the Romans ate horse-meat sausages. (Neigh! It's true!)

15 For vegetables, the Romans used some pretty odd things. Would you have eaten a salad made with dandelion leaves? How about an egg custard made with nettles? Or perhaps you'd prefer some stewed seaweed? These things are still eaten today in various parts of the world.

16 Sometimes, Roman banquet guests would drop rose petals into their wine.

17 At one meal, Heliogabalus served his guests 600 ostrich brains.

18 He also served peas mixed with grains of gold, and lentils mixed with precious stones – perhaps they liked rich food!

19 A favourite game was to disguise food so that it looked like something it wasn't! At one feast, roast piglets turned out to be made of pastry. At another, a nest seemed to be filled with eggs – but the eggs were made of pastry and inside, the "yolks" were made of spiced garden-warbler meat.

20 You might enjoy a meal while watching television. But could you eat at a Roman feast with dancers and acrobats, jugglers and clowns rushing around? Or even a pair of gladiators trying to kill each other?

The rotten Romans' daily diet

The main meals of the day for the Romans in Britain were:

MENU

BREAKFAST
BREAD AND FRUIT

LUNCH (PRANDIUM)
COLD EGGS, FISH OR VEGETABLES

DINNER (CENA)
GUSTATIO — TASTY THINGS LIKE RADISHES OR
ASPARAGUS AS A STARTER.
PRIMAE MENSALA — THE MAIN COURSE ; CHICKEN OR
HARE AND FISH AND VEGETABLE DISHES.
SECUNDAE MENSAE — SWEET COURSE, INCLUDING
FRUIT

Customer ID: ******9819

Items that you have renewed

Title: Rotten Romans
ID: 9018155365
Due: 15 March 2023

Total items: 1
Account balance: £0.00
22/02/2023 17:23
Borrowed: 1
Overdue: 0
Reservations: 0
Ready for collection: 0

Thank you for using Haltemprice Library
and Customer Services

01482 393939

Free eAudiobooks
Free eBooks
Free eMagazines

eastridinglibraries.co.uk/libraries-online

Rotten Roman beastly banquet

Why not invite your friends to a Roman-style banquet. Or, even better, invite your enemies.

First get your slaves to lay the table with a napkin, a spoon and a knife for each guest. No forks, you will notice. If you want to try a Roman banquet then you'll have to eat with your fingers and have a napkin to keep your fingers clean! For the soft food and sauces you can use a spoon, and a knife for cutting or spearing meat.

Before you start, place some of your food in a small bowl in front of the statue of the family god. (If the god doesn't eat it then the slaves will!)

Say a few prayers. The Romans would say, "Auguste, patri patriae" – "Good luck to the emperor, father of our country."

Have your slaves wash and dry the feet of your guests. (If you can't find any slaves at the local supermarket or corner shop then you could always use a parent or teacher.)

Warning:

Do not cook this food yourself! Have it done for you by your slaves!

Starter (Gustatio)

If your local shop doesn't have stuffed dormice or snails fattened in milk, then you may like to try shellfish, hard-boiled eggs or a dish of olives. Serve with spiced wine – or in your case, grape juice!

SPICED WINE

INGREDIENTS:
- 1 LITRE OF GRAPE JUICE
- 3 TABLESPOONS OF HONEY
- MIXED SPICE
- CINNAMON
- NUTMEG
- BLACK PEPPER
- WATER

METHOD:
- POUR GRAPE JUICE INTO A 2-LITRE SERVING JUG
- ADD A LITRE OF WATER – LESS IF YOU LIKE YOUR WINE STRONG.
- STIR IN THE HONEY TILL IT DISSOLVES.
- ADD A PINCH OF MIXED SPICE, ONE OF NUTMEG, CINNAMON AND BLACK PEPPER.
- TASTE IT AND ADD MORE HONEY IF IT'S NOT SWEET ENOUGH OR SPICES IF YOU WANT IT TASTIER.

Main Course (Primae Mensala)

NUMIDIAN CHICKEN

INGREDIENTS:
- CHICKEN PIECES (1 FOR EACH PERSON)
- CUMIN POWDER (QUARTER TEASPOON)
- CORIANDER SEEDS (QUARTER TEASPOON)
- 4 DATES (CHOPPED INTO SMALL PIECES)
- CHOPPED NUTS (4 TABLESPOONS)
- HONEY (2 TABLESPOONS)
- WINE VINEGAR (2 TABLESPOONS)
- CHICKEN STOCK (1 CHICKEN STOCK CUBE CRUMBLED IN A CUP OF WATER)
- PEPPER (A PINCH)
- COOKING OIL (1 TABLESPOON)
- BREAD CRUMBS (1 SLICE OF DRY BREAD)

METHOD:
- PUT THE CHICKEN PIECES IN A ROASTING DISH. BRUSH THEM WITH COOKING OIL, SPRINKLE THEM WITH PEPPER AND COVER THE DISH WITH COOKING FOIL. ROAST THE PIECES AT 350°F, 180°C OR GAS MARK 4 FOR HALF AN HOUR.
- WHILE THE CHICKEN IS ROASTING, PUT THE OTHER INGREDIENTS INTO A PAN AND SIMMER FOR TWENTY MINUTES TO MAKE NUMIDIAN SAUCE.
- WHEN THE CHICKEN PIECES ARE READY, PUT THEM ON A SERVING DISH AND POUR OVER THE SAUCE
- SERVE THE CHICKEN WITH VEGETABLES – CABBAGES AND BEANS ARE VERY ROMAN.

Sweet Course (Secundae Mensae)

DATES COOKED IN HONEY

INGREDIENTS:
- 12 FRESH DATES*
- 12 HALF WALNUTS
- 4 TABLESPOONS HONEY
- SALT
- BLACK PEPPER

   (*IF YOU CAN'T GET FRESH DATES THEN A PACKET
   OF COOKING DATES WILL DO)

METHOD:
- PEEL THE DATES AND TAKE OUT THE STONES.
- REPLACE EACH STONE WITH A HALF WALNUT.
- SPRINKLE EACH DATE LIGHTLY WITH SALT.
- MELT THE HONEY IN A PAN AND GENTLY COOK THE DATES IN THE HONEY.
- AFTER COOKING FOR FIVE MINUTES, TAKE OUT THE DATES AND ARRANGE ON A SERVING DISH.
- SPOON MORE HONEY OVER THE HOT DATES.
- SPRINKLE ON A LITTLE BLACK PEPPER AND SERVE.

Finish off with fruit and nuts and grape-juice wine. While eating your meal, have some entertainment from jugglers, dancers, singers or musicians.

It isn't polite to talk too much at a Roman banquet. But if you must talk, then don't chatter about common things — football, fashion or the neighbour's new car — talk about important things like life, death and great teachers of our time.

Rotten Roman remedies

It didn't do to be sick in Roman times. Sometimes the cure was worse than the illness! Here's a letter from a Roman, Cassius, to his sister, Juliet. Would you like to try some of his cures…?

DEAREST JULIET

I HAVE BEEN VERY WORRIED EVER SINCE I GOT YOUR LETTER TELLING ME THAT YOR WERE BITTEN BY A SPIDER HIDDEN AMONG THE VEGETABLES FROM THE GARDEN. IN APULIA THERE ARE A LOT OF DANGEROUS SPIDERS CALLED TARANTULAS. THE BEST REMEDY FOR THIER BITE IS, AS YOU KNOW, TO CRUSH THE BODY OF THE SPIDER ON THE WOUND. IF THAT IS IMPOSSIBLE THEN COVER THE SPOT WITH A PIECE OF ITS WEB.

ALTHOUGH YOU TELL ME YOU ARE BETTER I ADVISE YOU TO COME TO ROME AS SOON AS YOU CAN. WE WILL GO TOGETHER TO MAKE A SACRIFICE AT THE TEMPLE OF THE GODDESS CYBELE.

THERE ARE ALSO SOME USEFUL REMEDIES USING FROGS AS INGREDIENTS. A BROTH MADE OF SHRIMPS, FLOUR AND FROGS, BOILED IN WINE IS EXCELLENT FOR ANYONE WHO HAS LOST WEIGHT AND IS SUFFERING FROM TIREDNESS. CRUSHED FROGS, SOAKED IN WINE, ARE GOOD AGAINST THE POISONING OF TOADS.

FINALLY, TO CURE THE KIND OF FEVER WHICH COMES AROUND EVERY FOUR DAYS, YOU SHOULD EAT THE FLESH OF FROGS COOKED IN OLIVE OIL.

GIVE MY GREETINGS TO YOUR HUSBAND AND MY GOOD WISHES TO YOURSELF

YOUR LOVING BROTHER,

CASSIUS

Rotten Roman Religions

The Romans brought their religion and their gods with them from Rome, though in time they became mixed with the native British religions.

Lucky charms and cruel curses

In the Roman home the Lares were very important. These were household gods. They protected the home from evil spirits. In richer homes, Romans would also worship gods like...

Vesta – goddess of the fire and hearth ... and you can still buy matches called "Vestas"!

Penates – guardian of the store cupboard ... made sure nobody sneaked any midnight feasts.

Janus – the two-faced god who used his two faces to watch the people coming into the house and those going out.

The hot spring waters in the city of Bath are used as cures for all sorts of illnesses by people today. They were used by the Romans too. The Romans were a bit superstitious and believed there was magic in the water. They threw things into the water to take advantage of its powers. They threw coins in probably as you would into a wishing well – 12,000 Roman coins have been found there.

They also threw in written tablets, usually trying to make a deal with a god – "You do this for me, god, and I'll build an altar for you, OK?"

Many of these requests were for curses – if the name of the person you wanted to curse was written backwards, then the magic would be even stronger.

One man lost his girlfriend, Vilbia, to another man. He scratched the curse on a piece of metal … but wrote it backwards. Then he threw it in the water where it was found hundreds of years later. It read…

RETAW EKIL DIUQIL OTNI NRUT OT EM MORF
AIBLIV KOOT OHW NOSREP EHT TNAW I

(Do you know anyone you'd like to turn into a real drip?)

An even nastier curse has been found in Clothall. It was nailed on to some object, perhaps a dead animal, and says …

TACITA IS CURSED BY THIS AND WILL BE
DECAYED LIKE ROTTING BLOOD.

The rottenest Roman religions
Chucking chickens

The Roman army had its own religions and its own superstitions. The General of an army would look at the liver of certain animals, such as chickens, for signs as to how a battle might go. They might also…

• observe the flight of birds – the ways in which crows flew, for example.

• observe the way the sacred chickens ate their food – Claudius Pulcher took chickens with him on a voyage to the Punic Wars. The chickens were probably a bit seasick, because they refused to eat at all – a bad sign. So Claudius Pulcher ordered them to be thrown overboard with the words, "If they won't eat then let them drink!" He went on to lose the battle and the soldiers blamed him for drowning the sacred chickens!

I'M FEELING A LOT HUNGRIER NOW!

Stomach signals

A Roman teacher, Fronto, wrote to his pupil, Marcus, with news that he had a pain in the stomach. He believed this was a sign from the gods that there was bad luck coming to his family. (If your teacher had a pain in the stomach, she'd be more likely to blame school dinners!)

Mighty Mithras

The religion of the bull-god Mithras, was very popular with many Roman soldiers. He was probably brought to Britain by the legionaries who served in Persia, where Mithras was a popular god.

Mithras was the "judge" of the afterlife – he decided who should go to heaven and who should go to hell after they died.

The temples of Mithras were dark and gloomy places – sometimes underground – and a lot of the soldiers must have enjoyed joining this religion, because it was like joining a secret society.

You couldn't enter the temples until you'd performed certain brave deeds – like allowing yourself to be locked up for several hours in a coffin! The base of the coffin was on the stone-cold floor and the side was close to a fire – you froze and fried at the same time!

I CAN ONLY LET YOU IN ONCE YOU'VE TOLD ME THE SECRET PASSWORD, SHOWN ME YOUR SECRET RING, GIVEN ME THE SECRET HANDSHAKE, AND..ER..FOUND THE KEY

Bull's blood

Another Eastern "mystery" religion had equally gruesome rituals, as Prudentius described in the 4th century AD...

> *"The worshippers dig a deep pit and the High Priest is lowered into it. Above him they put a platform of loose planks. Each plank has tiny holes drilled in it. A huge bull is stood on the platform. They take a sacred hunting spear and drive it into the bull's*

heart. The hot blood spurts out
of the deep wound. It falls
through the holes in the planks
like rotten rain on to the priest
below. His clothes and body
are covered in the animal's
gore. Afterwards he climbs out
of the pit. It is a dreadful sight
to see. 🙶

Christianity

From the end of the first century AD, Christianity began to enter Britain. After the exciting Roman religions some Christians seemed a bit boring. One Christian writer, Tertullian, was against fancy clothes – he didn't even like to see them dyed. He wrote…

If God had wanted us to wear purple and sky-blue clothes, then He would have given us purple and sky-blue sheep!

By AD **250**, the emperors began stamping out Christianity and killing Christians. St Alban was one of the victims in Britain. Still, Christianity continued to grow there.

Then, in AD **313**, the Act of Toleration was passed that allowed Christians to worship openly. But it was all too late for poor old Alban...

PURPLE? WITH ALL THAT GREEN GRASS AROUND? WE'D CLASH!

The legend of St Alban

The wind blew wild and wet along the wall. Two soldiers shivered behind their shields and complained.

"End of the world, this place. End of the world!" old Laganus groaned.

"Not quite the end of the world," his young partner pointed out. "There are people on the other side of the wall."

"People!" Laganus laughed. "Them Picts aren't *people*. More what you'd call *animals*. Proper people wouldn't live out in that wild country. They're *savages*, Paul, *savages*."

Young Paul huddled into his cloak and looked across the bleak and empty moors. "Not as savage as the Romans can be," he said carefully.

"That's no way to talk about our masters!"

184

Laganus gasped. "That's the sort of talk that'll get you beaten!"

Paul nodded. "That's what I mean. They'll beat me. They're cruel."

The older man snorted. "You're just soft, my boy. You've got to kill your enemy. Kill or get yourself killed. That's the way it is!"

"You wouldn't say that if you were a Christian," Paul told him.

Laganus turned on him savagely. "Yeh! I've heard all about your Christian God! Look at that Alban!"

"They killed him!" Paul cried. "The Romans killed him!"

"But that's nothing to what your kind and gentle God did for revenge, is it?" the old soldier sneered.

He sat down in the shelter of the wall and rubbed his freezing hands. "I heard the true story from a soldier of the Seventh Legion last week."

Paul crouched down beside him. "Alban was a hero. A Christian martyr…"

"Alban was a soldier just like you or me. Well, more like you, Paul. He was soft-hearted. Soft in the head too, if you ask me. The Romans were having one of their crackdowns on the Christians. You know the sort of thing. Killing a few here and there to show them who is boss."

"Murder," Paul muttered.

"Alban was a *Roman* soldier, of course. He should have been joining in the *killing* of the Christians. Instead he gave *shelter* to a Christian priest."

"Amphibalus," the young soldier nodded.

"And worse! He let this Amphibalus talk *him* into becoming a Christian!" Laganus groaned. "They sent soldiers to arrest Alban, of course. What did he do? Disguised himself and tried to run away."

"They caught him," Paul sighed.

"Of course they caught him! But they didn't kill him for hiding the enemy – they didn't kill him for becoming a Christian..."

"They did!" Paul cut in.

"No, no, no! They gave him a chance. They told him to make a sacrifice to the Roman gods. Prove that he was still loyal!" the old soldier said.

"He refused."

"So it serves him right if he was sentenced to death," Laganus snorted. "But the Romans didn't have him tortured or crucified or stoned to death. No. They were kind. They sentenced him to a quick death by beheading!"

"They murdered him," Paul repeated stubbornly.

"Ah, but that was quick and kind. What happened at the execution, eh? You Christians never tell about that!"

The young soldier shrugged. "I don't know."

Laganus grinned. Two soldiers led Alban to the place of execution. Alban managed to convert one of them on the way. But he didn't convert the second one, did he? The second executioner cut off Alban's head! *Then* your 'kind', kind God took his cruel, cruel revenge. As Alban's head hit the ground the executioner staggered back clutching his face. When the guards reached him they found that his eyes had both dropped out! Plop! Plop!"

By the end of that century, Christianity became the religion of the Roman State. But some parts of the British Isles were converted as the result of a strange accident...

Pirates, pagans and Patrick

Did you know?

I Patrick is the patron saint of Ireland, BUT he was born in Wales, lived in England and his parents were Roman.

2 When he was 16 he was kidnapped by Celtic pirates and taken as a slave to Ireland.

3 He was given a rotten job by the Irish pagans
– looking after cattle on the bleak hills.

4 A boulder crashed down the mountainside
towards Patrick. Just before it flattened him it
split in two. One piece went on either side of
him.

5 Patrick took this as a miracle. He believed it
was a sign from God that there was special
work for him.

6 He escaped to Gaul, then returned home to
become a farmer. He still felt that his life had
been saved for some special reason.

7 He boldly went back to Ireland.

8 He performed miracles there. There is a story, for example, that there are no snakes in Ireland because Patrick got rid of them all.

9 Patrick converted the kings of many Irish kingdoms to Christianity. The kings were baptized and the people followed the kings.

10 A king of southern Ireland had a rotten baptism. Patrick carried a crook – like a shepherd. It was pointed on the bottom. During the baptism Patrick accidentally put the point clean through the king's foot. The king didn't complain; he thought it was all part of the ceremony.

Rotten Roman Facts

The rottenest Roman historian

At the eastern end of the Roman Wall is a fort. In 1971 the museum at the fort proudly showed their latest find. "It is a sestertius coin, made between AD 135 and AD 138. On the back of the coin is a large letter 'R' – standing for Roma," they said.

Then an expert, Miss Fiona Gordon, told them they were wrong. The sestertius was, in fact, a free gift given away with bottles of fruit squash. "The letter 'R' stands for the name of the makers, Robinson!"

The museum keepers discovered Miss Gordon was correct. That was embarrassing! But, most embarrassing of all, Miss Fiona Gordon was just nine years old!

True or false?

1 A favourite method of execution in ancient Rome was "stinging to death".

2 The Roman Fort at Sinodum is supposed to be the site of a money-pit full of buried treasure.

3 Druids picked their victims by going "Eeny-meeny-miney-mo..."

REMIND ME, WHAT COMES AFTER MO?

4 Women could be Druids.

5 Druids would stab a victim in the back, then see the future from the way he died.

6 A crash at a chariot race was called "a plane-crash".

7 The Victorians pulled down the east end of Hadrian's Wall and used the stone to mend their roads.

8 The Romans didn't have peppermint toothpaste. They preferred powdered mouse-brains.

9 The Romans stopped traffic jams in Aldborough by building a bypass.

THIS ONE I'LL CALL A FLYOVER

10 In Roman horse races the losing horse was killed.

Answers

1 True – the victim was smothered in honey then covered with angry wasps.

2 True – in the 19th century a local villager was digging at the fort one day when he came across an iron chest. A raven landed on it and said, "He is not born yet!" The villager thought this meant, "The person who can open the chest is not yet born." He filled the hole in and left. Are you the one born to open the chest?

3 True – according to Victorian experts. The shepherds of ancient Britain would count sheep with a number system that sounded very like "Eeny-meeny-miney-mo". The Druids could well have used it. Children may then have copied it as part of a gruesome game and it's been used in children's games ever since.

4 True – the Romans said that they met Druidesses. These women were good at telling fortunes.

5 True – the Roman historian, Strabo, said the way a man twisted and fell after he had been stabbed helped a Druid to read the fortunes for his tribe.

6 False – it was called a "shipwreck".

7 True. There are still large stretches of Hadrian's Wall to be seen across the north of England. It's well looked after now … but it hasn't always been. Farmers pinched stones from the Wall to build their houses, and the Victorians were worse. They pulled the wall down, smashed up the stones into little bits and used them to repair the roads of Newcastle!

8 True – perhaps they wanted their teeth to be "squeaky" clean! They also used powdered horn, oyster-shell ash and the ashes of dogs' teeth mixed with honey.

9 True.

10 False – the winning horse was killed as a sacrifice to the god of war, Mars. The local people often fought fiercely to decide who would have the honour of sticking its head on their wall.

Rotten Roman towns

Everyone tells you about how marvellous the Roman baths were. But not all of the Romans were so keen. One Roman wrote…

I live above the public baths, and we all know what that means. Yeuch! It's sickening. Firstly there are the strong men doing exercises, swinging lead weights round with grunts and groans. Then there are the lazy ones having a cheap massage – I can hear them being slapped on the back. Then there are the noises of fighters and thieves being arrested. Worst is the sound of the man who likes to hear his own voice in the bath. And what about the ones who leap into the bath and make a huge splash in the water?

SPLASH

LA LA LA

LA LA

SLAP

CHATTER CHATTER

GROAN

ONE TWO ONE TWO

SLAP SLAP

GRUNT

OW!

Rotten Romans today

The rotten Romans ran
the world for a long time.
There are still signs of
their life today.

Did you know?

1 The Romans signed their "trademark" wherever they went. They wrote the letters SPQR, which stood for Senatus Populus Que Romanus – The Senate and the People of Rome. The buses and the drain covers of Rome have the letters on them today.

2 The Roman language is called Latin. It is still used in some religious ceremonies and used to be taught in many schools. But no one speaks it as an everyday language now. So it's called a "dead" language. That's why schoolchildren who still have to learn it mutter the same old school chant…

LATIN IS A LANGUAGE
AS DEAD AS DEAD CAN BE
IT KILLED THE ANCIENT BRITONS-
AND NOW IT'S KILLING ME!

3 Much of the Roman Wall can still be seen – and walked along – in the north of England. But the famous historian and monk, St Bede, got his facts about Hadrian's Wall completely wrong! He said the Romans built it just before they abandoned Britain. It was a sort of farewell present for the Britons, planned to keep the Picts and Scots out. He wrote…

"When the Wall was finished, the Romans gave clear advice to the dejected Britons, then said goodbye to their friends and never returned. The gloomy British soldiers lived in terror day and night. Beyond the Wall the enemy constantly attacked them with hooked weapons, dragging the defenders down from the Wall and dashing them to the ground. At last the Britons abandoned their cities and the Wall and fled in confusion."

Wrong! The Wall was there 300 years before the Romans left. Don't believe everything you read in history books – even if the writer is a saint!

4 There are some rotten things in Britain today that we can blame the Romans for. They brought them here. Things like…

• stinging nettles – next time you sit on one, you can cry out in agony, "Oooh! The rotten Romans!"

• cabbages and peas – the sort of vegetables your parents make you eat because "they're good for you." Next time you hear that, you can say, "The ancient Britons survived a few million years without them!"

• cats – yes, blame the Romans for that mangy moggy that yowls all night on the corner of your street and keeps you awake. When teacher tells you off for yawning in class, say, "Don't blame me – blame the rotten Romans!"

5 Rotten spelling – a lot of the words we use today come from Latin. They made sense to the rotten Romans but they don't make sense to us. Take the Latin word "plumbum"... no, it doesn't mean purple bottom. It means waterworks. So we get a word for a man who fixes your leaky waterworks from that. That's right, "plumber". We say it "plummer" and any sensible Briton in their right mind would spell it "plummer". But the Romans put that useless "b" in the middle, so we have to. Next time you get two out of ten for your spelling test say, "Don't blame me – blame the rotten Romans!"

6 False teeth – the Romans generally had good teeth. They cleaned them regularly and didn't have sugar to rot them. But, if they did lose a tooth, they used false teeth. These would be made of gold or ivory. They'd be held in place with gold wire. That wire could also be used to hold loose teeth in place. The poor people just had to let them drop out.

Ancient Roman ancient joke:

DOCTOR DOCTOR! HAVE YOU GOT SOMETHING TO KEEP MY TEETH IN?

CERTAINLY, MADAM, HERE'S A PAPER BAG!

7 Skyscrapers – the Romans made buildings with more floors than anyone else of their age. But this led to some rotten Roman tragedies. In 217 BC an ox escaped from the local market. It ran into a three-storey building and up the stairs. When it reached the top it threw itself out of a window on the top floor. By the time of Augustus the crowded cities were forcing people to build houses higher and higher – a bit like Britain in the 1960s! But many of these tower blocks began to collapse – so Augustus passed a law banning any building over 20 metres tall.

8 A family living in Hertford, England, are so keen on the Romans that they eat Roman food (like sardines stuffed with dates – yeuch!) and play Roman games after dinner. The family have organized a new Fourteenth Legion (but with only 24 legionaries so far) who go on 40-kilometre marches just as the original legion did. They also dress as Romans occasionally and go around schools to give demonstrations to children. This does not always have the desired result – sometimes younger pupils see the Roman soldier walk into the classroom and they burst into tears … usually the boys! Oh, and the daughter of the family isn't a fan of the Romans and is too embarrassed by her Roman family to bring her boyfriend home!

9 We have Christmas traditions today that live on from Roman times. One tradition is Roman and one British. They were…

• holly – the Romans had ceremonies for their god, Saturn, in December. The decoration they used was holly. Country people still believe that it's a protection against poison, storms, fire and "the evil eye".

• mistletoe – trees were sacred to the Britons. Mistletoe grew on trees and sucked the spirit from them – that's the sticky juice in the berries. The oak was the most sacred tree, so mistletoe from the oak was the most precious plant of all. Druids in white robes cut it with golden knives on the sixth day of a new moon. A sprig over the door protected the house from thunder, lightning and all evil.

10 Christianity put an end to the Druids' human sacrifices ... but 2,000 years later we may still have curious memories of those deadly days ... the children's game London Bridge is Falling Down. Some form of this game is known all over the world.

Two children link hands and form an arch. The rest of the children have to pass under the arch while chanting the song. When a child is caught, then the bridge has fallen. That child becomes the "watchman" of the bridge.

But the legends say that, in the days of pagan beliefs, the unlucky child could only guard the bridge if he (or she) was dead! It seems the spirits of rivers hate bridges and without a sacrifice they would bring it down. The British legend says that children were sacrificed and their blood poured over the stones of the first London Bridge to keep "Old Father Thames" happy.

Epilogue

The Romans left to defend their homeland and Rome. The Britons were left to defend the island against enemies old and new. A historian from those times, Gildas, described how the "foul" Picts and Scots with their "lust for blood" swarmed over Hadrian's mighty Wall. They pulled the British defenders down from the Wall and killed them like "lambs are slaughtered by butchers". The men from the north with their hairy "hang-dog" faces took over.

Four hundred years before, the Britons had fought the Romans off. But in four hundred years the Britons had forgotten how to fight. Suddenly the Romans didn't seem so rotten after all. Now the Britons wrote and begged them to return...

❝The barbarians drive us to the sea, the sea drives us back to the barbarians. Between these two methods of death we are either massacred or drowned.❞

But no help came. Rome had problems of its own. After hundreds of years of Roman rule, Britain entered "The Dark Ages".

IT WAS ROTTEN HAVING THE ROMANS HERE

YEAH... I WISH THEY'D COME BACK THOUGH

ROTTEN ROMANS

Quiz

Evil emperors

It's really weird but true. Some of the battiest people in history have been leaders – kings and queens, emperors and empresses, presidents and princes. It's almost as if you have to be slightly potty to be a ruler!

Rome had their fair share of rotten rulers. Here are a few foul facts about them. Only the odd word has been left out for you to complete…

Here are the missing words, in the wrong order: mother, head, chicken, horse, corpse, cobweb, cheese, wife, wrinkly, leg.

1 Augustus Caesar (31 BC–AD 14) caught Brutus, the murderer of Julius Caesar, and had his _____ thrown at the feet of Caesar's statue.

2 Tiberius (AD 14–37) said that he would smash the _____ of anyone who disobeyed him.

3 Caligula (AD 37–41) wanted someone to help him to rule so he gave the job to his _____.

4 Claudius (AD 41–54) had his _____ executed.

5 Nero (AD 54–68) tried to drown his _____.

6 Vitellius (AD 69) had his _____ thrown in the River Tiber at Rome.

7 Hadrian (AD 117–138) forced a _____ to commit suicide.

8 Antonius (AD 138–161) died of eating too much

_____.

9 Heliogabalus (AD 218–222) had the curious hobby of collecting every _____ he could find.

10 Honorius (AD 395–423) had a _____ called "Rome".

Stabbing Jules

Julius Caesar was a brilliant Roman leader, but he became a bit too big for his boots – his red boots, in fact. The Romans were now used to having leaders who were "elected". They had hated their old kings ... who had worn red boots instead of a crown, but when the booted-up kings were kicked out the Romans got on much better with their elected leaders.

But Julius got himself elected for life. Just like a king. When he started wearing red boots, his number was up. There was just one way to get rid of him then – assassination.

His friend Brutus led the murderers, who struck when Caesar was entering the Roman parliament (the senate). Roman writer Plutarch told the gory story. Can you sort out the scrambled words in this version?

Some of Brutus's gang slipped behind Caesar's chair while others came to meet him. Cimber grabbed Caesar's robe and pulled it from his neck. This was the A SLING for the attack.

Casca struck the first blow. His IF KEN

217

made a wound in ASSA CRE's neck but Caesar was able to turn round, grab the knife and hold on. The HAT CREWS were horrified but didn't dare move or make a sound.

Each AS SINS AS bared his dagger now. They pushed Caesar this way and that like a wild BE SAT surrounded by hunters.

Brutus stabbed Caesar in the groin. Above all Caesar had RED TUTS Brutus. When he saw Brutus coming towards him he pulled his robe over his head and sank down.

The attackers pushed Caesar against the ASTUTE of his old enemy Pompey. The statue became drenched with DO LOB.

Caesar received 23 wounds. Many of the assassins WON DUDE each other as they fought to stick so many knives into one body.

Foul Roman food

Do you know what the rotten Romans ate? Have a go at this quirky quiz on cuisine (that's a posh word for "cooking") and find out…

1 The Romans didn't have tomato ketchup but they did have sauce made from what?

a sheep eyeballs

b fish guts

c elephant's tail

MY HAMBURGER IS BLINKING!

2 At posh Roman feasts guests sometimes ate more than their stomachs could hold. How?

a They emptied their stomachs by vomiting every now and then.

b They stretched their stomachs with special exercises.

c They stuck a pin in their stomach to let out trapped air and let in more food.

3 Snails were fattened up before they were killed. They were kept in a bowl of what?

a chopped cabbage

b brains

c blood

4 Emperor Heliogabalus also served a meal where the peas were mixed with what?

a queues

b poison

c gold nuggets

5 Emperor Heliogabalus served 600 of them at one feast. What?

a ostrich brains

b ducks' feet

c camel-burgers

6 A Roman called Trimalchio had a feast with a roasted boar. When it was sliced down the belly, what came out?

a maggots

b songbirds

c a dancing girl

7 What could you watch as you ate at some Roman feasts?

a television

b two gladiators trying to murder one another

c tap-dancing bears

TICKETTY TICKETTY TICKETTY

TICKETTY TICKETTY TICKETTY

8 The Romans ate cute little pets that you probably wouldn't eat. What?

a cats

b budgies

c dormice

9 The Romans did not eat animals' what?

a teeth

b brains

c lungs

10 Emperor Maximian was a strange eater. Why?

a He was the only vegetarian emperor.

b He ate only eggs and drank only water.

c He ate 20 kilos of meat a day.

Answers

Evil emperors

1 head. Nice present for Jules!

2 leg. Tiberius died at the age of 77, probably suffocated by his chief helper.

3 horse. Cruel Caligula liked to feed criminals to wild animals. He was stabbed to death by one of his guards.

4 wife. She was a bit of a flirt. But he also had 300 of her party friends chopped too! His third wife and niece had him poisoned with mushrooms.

5 mother. When the plot failed he sent soldiers to give her the chop. Nero stabbed himself to death before his enemies got to him.

6 corpse. He was murdered in the centre of Rome but not given a nice emperor's burial.

7 wrinkly. Hadrian accused Servianus of treason and forced him to kill himself. But Servianus was 90 years old and hardly a big threat.

8 cheese. At least that's what a Roman historian blamed his death on. Guess it was just hard cheese.

WHY NOT TRY *THIS* CHEESE, YOUR IMPERIAL LOFTINESS?

9 cobweb. Maybe he was planning to build the world's first website?

10 chicken. Trouble is he loved the chicken Rome more than he loved the city Rome, and the city was neglected.

Stabbing Jules

These are the unscrambled words in the correct order: signal; knife; Caesar's; watchers; assassin; beast; trusted; statue; blood; wounded.

Foul Roman food

1b The guts were soaked in salt water and left to stew in the sun for a few days. Then the fish-gut sauce was poured over the food as a tasty treat. Oh my cod!

2a They used a stick with a feather to tickle their tonsils and vomited into a bowl. When their stomach was empty they went back and ate more. Scoff-vomit, scoff-vomit, scoff-vomit all night long.

3cThe snails supped the blood till they were too fat to get in their shells. The blood diet made them taste nice. If they wanted creamy snails, the Romans fed them on milk before eating them.

4c Heliogabalus mixed gold and precious stones with the peas as a sort of treat. But if one of those diamonds smashed your teeth you'd be sore. And if you swallowed a gold nugget you'd be ill! You'd have to sit on the toilet and wait for some change!

5a Ostrich brains are quite small so he'd need 600 to keep his guests fed. But where did he get all those ostriches? Zoo knows?

6b There were thrushes stuffed inside the roast boar. (Were they bored in there?) Trimalchio also served wine that was 100 years old at that feast.

THESE WERE THE ONLY BIRDS WE COULD GET

7b Of course, the trouble with gladiators fighting as you eat is that they could splash blood and guts all over your freshly cooked dinner. Aren't you lucky you don't suffer that while you watch telly?

8c They fed the dormice really well on walnuts, acorns and chestnuts. They were served roasted and stuffed with pork sausage. Scrummy! Even tastier than hamster or gerbil!

9a They ate all sorts of other things though. As well as sheep and goat lungs or brains, they ate gulls, peacocks, swans and jackdaws. They stuffed the birds just by pushing stuffing straight down their throats. They didn't clean the insides out the way you do with your Christmas turkey. Yeuch!

10c That's about a small sheep every day. Would ewe believe it? He was also supposed to have drunk about 18 bottles of wine ... but it must have been very weak. Of course, after 20 years all that eating killed him, but he was probably too drunk to notice he was dead!

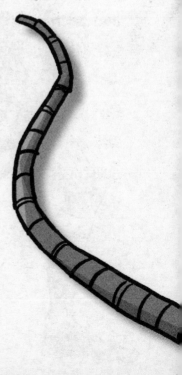

CUT-THROAT CELTS

History is horrible. Especially in school. Have you noticed how teachers never *tell* you anything? They *ask* you something and expect you to *know*!

THE CELTS LIVED IN THE IRON AGE. WHAT'S THE IRON AGE, CILLA?

WELL, MY MUM SAYS IT TAKES AN AGE TO DO THE IRONING!

They use funny new words and ask you to guess what they mean! How on earth can they expect that?

And they use posh words to describe the really horrible bits of history…

Then, just when there's a chance that history lessons may be getting interesting, the teacher stops and refuses to tell you the gory details.

BUT WHAT DID THEY DO WITH THE HEADS WHEN THEY'D EVAPORATED THEM?

THE WORD IS DECAPITATED. NOW GET ON WITH YOUR WRITING

Were the Celts really cut-throats? And why? And what did they do with those heads? What you need is a book that tells you the truth, the whole truth and nothing but the truth. What you need is a Horrible History of the cut-throat Celts!

Well! You lucky person! You just happen to have found one...

Cut-throat Celt Timeline

750 BC

The ancient Greeks meet traders from Hallstatt (Austria). The Greeks say they call themselves **Keltoi** – dodgy spelling, but better

than the Celts who can't write at all!

387 BC

Now the Celts meet the Romans and beat them in battle. The Romans – also dodgy spellers – call them **Celtae**.

279 BC

The Greeks drive the Celts out of Greece after the Battle of **Delphi**. The Greeks have the help of bad weather and landslides (which is cheating a bit).

225 BC

At the Battle of **Telemon** in Greece the Romans beat the Celts.

218 BC

The **Carthaginians** of North Africa attack the Romans in Italy and the Celts help them but...

202 BC

The Romans beat the Carthaginians in Carthage and turn their attention to Celt lands in Spain and Northern Italy. Sweet Roman **revenge**.

60 BC

Roman **Julius Caesar** decides to make a name for himself by taking over Celtic Gaul (France). Some Celts welcome him – others don't ... and are wiped out.

52 BC

Vercingetorix leads a Celtic rebellion against Caesar. Romans win and rule France. Then they start looking across the English Channel…

AD 43

Emperor Claudius defeats the Celts in Britain. They're driven back to the hills of Wales and Scotland despite…

AD 61

A very bloody rebellion led by **Queen Boudicca** ends in another win for the Romans.

AD **84**

Battle of **Mons Graupius** in Scotland, and the last of the free Celts are now in Scotland and Ireland. The Romans rule, OK?

AD **120**

Emperor Hadrian
builds a wall across the
north of England to keep
the **Pict** and Scot Celts
out ... or to keep them
in, depending on which
way you look at it!

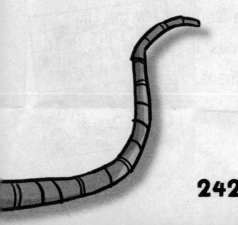

AD 312

Emperor Constantine
becomes a Christian and the
Roman Empire converts to
Christianity. Even the Celts
are converted and their old
ways die. No more sacrifices.

AD 410

The Romans leave Britain but **Angles**, **Saxons**
and **Jutes** rush in and settle before the free Celts
can get back. A bit like musical chairs!

AD **432**

St Patrick goes to Ireland and converts Irish Celts to Christianity.

AD **493**

The British Celts make one last effort to drive out the Saxons and win the Battle of Badon. Their leader is the awesome **King Arthur** ... maybe.

AD 520

Awesome Arthur loses his last battle when he fights his own nephew ... maybe. But while the British Celts are squabbling, the Angles and Saxons take over the south-east of Britain and create Angle-land, or **England**. You may have heard of it.

Getting to Know the Cut-throat Celts

The thing that made them Celts was that they shared a language and they shared their legends and their customs. The Romans might have ruled them ... but the Romans were still pretty scared of them!

THE CELTS ARE TERRIFYING IN APPEARANCE WITH DEEP-SOUNDING AND VERY HARSH VOICES. THEY USE FEW WORDS AND SPEAK IN RIDDLES. THEY OFTEN EXAGGERATE WITH THE AIM OF MAKING THEMSELVES LOOK GOOD AND MAKING OTHERS LOOK WEAK. THEY ARE BOASTERS AND THREATENERS, YET THEY HAVE QUICK MINDS AND A NATURAL ABILITY FOR LEARNING.

SAY I'M THE BEST OR I'LL BITE YOUR KNEECAPS OFF

Diodorus Siculus, 1st century BC

The largest Celt tribe that the Romans came up against were called Gauls…

ALMOST ALL OF THE GAULS ARE TALL, FAIR AND RED-FACED, TERRIBLE FOR THE FIERCENESS OF THEIR EYES, FOND OF QUARRELLING AND OF DREADFUL PRIDE.

GRRRR

Ammianus Marcellinus, 4th century AD

The Romans said some pretty spiteful things about the Celts, including…

WHEN THE CELTS BECOME DRUNK THEY FALL INTO A DEEP SLEEP ... OR THEY FALL INTO A TERRIBLE RAGE.

NOW I'M REALLY ANGRY

BUT I'M EVEN ANGRIER

ZZZ

Diodorus Siculus, 1st century BC

The ancient Celts were violent and loved arguing, but is it fair to call them "cut-throat"? Maybe. Look at the evidence and decide for yourself.

Guilty or not guilty?

THERE ARE STORIES ABOUT CELT WARRIORS INVADING A COUNTRY AND MARRYING ITS WOMEN. THEY SAY THE CELTS CUT OUT THE TONGUES OF THEIR NEW WIVES SO THE PURE LANGUAGE OF THE MEN WILL NOT BE SPOILED BY THE FOREIGN LANGUAGE OF THEIR NEW WIVES

THESE STORIES ARE FOUND ONLY IN LEGENDS BUT I CAN'T HELP WONDERING IF THE STORY-TELLERS HAD SOME TRUTH TO BASE THEIR GRUESOME TALES ON ...

PROVE IT

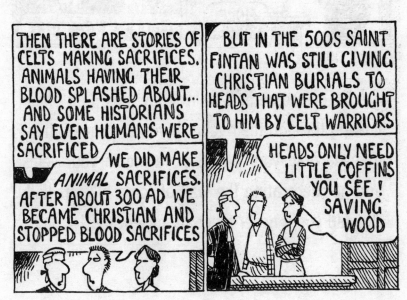

THEN THERE ARE STORIES OF CELTS MAKING SACRIFICES. ANIMALS HAVING THEIR BLOOD SPLASHED ABOUT... AND SOME HISTORIANS SAY EVEN HUMANS WERE SACRIFICED

WE DID MAKE *ANIMAL* SACRIFICES. AFTER ABOUT 300 AD WE BECAME CHRISTIAN AND STOPPED BLOOD SACRIFICES

BUT IN THE 500S SAINT FINTAN WAS STILL GIVING CHRISTIAN BURIALS TO HEADS THAT WERE BROUGHT TO HIM BY CELT WARRIORS

HEADS ONLY NEED LITTLE COFFINS YOU SEE! SAVING WOOD

A lot of people in Britain today have Celt blood flowing through their veins. If you are one of them then be glad your blood is staying in your veins and not decorating the wall of some hill fort hall. Be glad you'll never meet an ancient Celt!

Lousy Legends

Poets were highly respected in the Celt world — like pop singers today. And, like pop singers, they were well paid. The bad news is that it was a long hard job to train as a Celtic poet. A pop singer probably trains for 12 whole minutes — a Celtic poet trained for 12 years.

Poets learned grammar and very long poems — 80 in the first six years. They learned another 95 in the next three years, and by the end of the 12-years' training they would know 350 story-poems ... if they survived, that is.

Because learning a story-poem an hour or so long took a lot of concentration. Have you ever had a teacher complain that you lack concentration? Did they nag you into concentrating? Think yourself lucky – you could have had a Celtic poetry teacher.

The poet travelled round with a metal model of a tree branch. It had bells on and they rang as he rode along or entered a feasting hall.

The branch told you what sort of poet he was – a bronze branch for a qualified poet, a silver branch for an expert and a gold branch for someone who was top of the pops.

He'd swagger around in a cloak covered in birds' feathers – the feathers of white and coloured birds were worn below the belt, the crests and necks of mallard ducks above the belt. Some say a swan's head dangled down his back (don't try making one of these – you'll just look quackers).

The poet expected to be well paid for his entertainment. If he wasn't then he was likely to compose a very sarcastic verse about the lord in charge. You know the sort of thing…

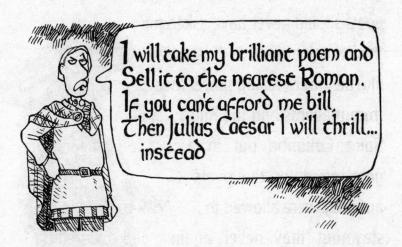

> I will take my brilliant poem and
> Sell it to the nearest Roman.
> If you can't afford me bill,
> Then Julius Caesar I will thrill…
> instead

Never upset a king...

Of course some poets became too greedy and in AD 574 King Aed Mac Ainmirech banned all poets from Ireland. The King had a symbol of his power – a brooch in the shape of a wheel. Some poets got a bit cheeky and asked him for it. Lords often gave pieces of jewellery for a good story but the poets should never have asked for the wheel brooch – it seemed like they were taking power away from the lords and the King. Saint Columba put in a good word for the poets and they were allowed to stay, but they never again asked for impossibly grand payments.

258

...and *never* upset a poet!

But be warned. It didn't pay to upset a poet. If he cursed you, you might...

- lose in battle
- break out in blisters
- speak only baby-talk.

MUMMY, MUMMY, THAT NASTY ARMY BEATED ME ALL UP, THEN I GOT BWISTERS ALL OVER

SOB

Terrible tales

Imagine the nastiest thing possible. That's the sort of thing the Celtic poets sang about. There's nothing wrong with the following story ... unless you're a member of the Pony Club and don't enjoy horse-burgers and chips.

Horses meant speed and beauty – they were linked to the Celtic Sun god. Celts believed that you could gain some of a horse's powers by eating it. (I've tried this. Does it work? Neigh!)

WARNING: Horse lovers should skip the following poem! It is loosely based on a Celtic poem ... very loosely. Well, to be honest, if it got any looser it would drop off.

The king was in his feasting house
Waiting to be crowned.
They killed a white horse, cut it up,
And stirred it round and round
Inside a cauldron great and deep
All filled with water, hot.
They ate the horse meat, not the bones,
Until they'd scoffed the lot.

(Well, when I say "the lot", I mean
They didn't eat the saddle.)
The king stood up, and then he cried,
"My friends! It's time we paddled!"
The king's friends all took off their
clothes
And jumped into the pot!
They splashed about in bones and soup,
And see how clean they got!

And when they all had washed and
scrubbed,
They jumped back out again.
They drank the horse soup, every drop
Until the pot was drained.

Not much wrong with eating horse meat — the French do it all the time. But would you drink bath-water after all your smelly friends have bathed in it? Yeuch!

Batty Beliefs

The Celts had gods all over the place – gods in trees, gods in streams and even gods in stones. The oak tree was especially holy and the mistletoe that grew on it was magical stuff. People today still believe this and that's why we have the Christmas custom of kissing under the mistletoe.

WARNING: Do not be tricked into kissing some snotty creep who happens to fancy you. Tell them the truth...

MISTLETOE IS ONLY MAGICAL WHEN IT IS CUT BY A DRUID USING A GOLD SICKLE

THAT MAKES *ME* SICKLE

Ten things you need to know about Druids

1 Laws were made by the kings, but it was the Druids who advised the king. This is rather like Government Ministers advising the Queen today. They are *her* laws – but everybody knows the Government runs the country. The Druids also acted as judges to enforce those laws. It didn't pay to upset a Druid.

2 Druids were clever clogs because they spent 20 years training to become one. This is even worse than modern schools where you spend 11 to 15 years training to be an adult. You then spend another 50 years wondering if it was worth it.

3 The sacred mistletoe must not touch the ground. When the Druid with the golden sickle climbed a tree, another two Druids stood below and caught it in a white cloth as he threw it down. (This was also very handy if the Druid with the golden sickle fell out of the tree!)

4 These Druids were the village wise men (and maybe wise women) who advised the villagers on problems like the best time to plant their crops.

They were like your local vicar but with an important difference. Your vicar might expect a five-pound note from each of his worshippers – a Druid expected blood. And the Druids had real power over the people. As Roman Julius Caesar said…

> WHEN A PERSON DISOBEYS A DRUID THEN THEY BAN THEM FROM ATTENDING AT SACRIFICES. THIS IS THE CRUELLEST PUNISHMENT A CELT CAN SUFFER.

5 The Roman writer, Lucan, said Druids even sacrificed humans. Lucan claimed that, "the trees were sprinkled with human blood." Yeuch. Of course Lucan could have been exaggerating a bit

... or a lot. The Romans didn't like the Celts and may have written a few lies about them. Of course the Celts didn't do much writing, so the Roman stories have gone down in history and the truth has been forgotten.

6 The Celts of Gaul sent their Druids over to Britain to be trained. British Celt Druids must have been the best.

268

7 When a Druid wanted some spirit help he slaughtered a bull and had it skinned. Then he lay down on a bed of rowan branches and wrapped the bull's hide round him, bloody side next to him. As he slept he experienced dreams that answered his questions or solved his people's problems — problems like, "How do you get blood stains out of a Druid's best robe?"

OF WHAT DID YOU DREAM O GREAT DRUID?

FOR SOME REASON, ALL THAT CAME INTO MY HEAD WAS LOADS OF FRESH HAY AND CHARGING AT RED THINGS

8 Druids were also fortune-tellers who said they could see into the future. What would you do if you could see into the future? Become a fortune-teller and make your fortune? Or simply pick next Saturday's winning lottery numbers – every week for a year? It's easy. All you have to do is follow the dreadful Druid method of divining the future.

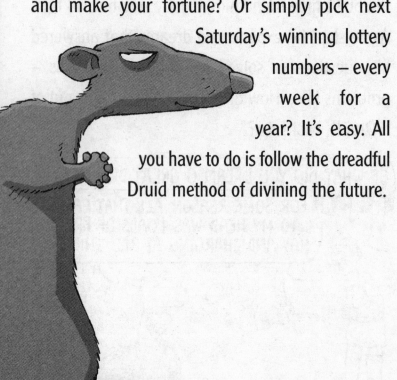

• Take the flesh of a dog.

• Chew it.

• Call upon the spirit of the dog to give you its secret.

• Have a long deep sleep OR place the palms of your hands over your eyes, crossing your hands over your face.

• A vision will reveal the wisdom that is guarded by the animal.

The Celtic Druids used this method to predict who the next king would be. But why would a wise dog know that? You may not be able to get the flesh of a dog – maybe next door's Rottweiler doesn't want you to bite its leg – but the Celts believed the flesh of a cat or a bull would give up that animal's secret. Could a cat's flesh reveal winning scratch cards? (Cat's – scratch … geddit? Oh, never mind.) Probably the flesh of a bull is easiest to get hold of. Chew that and soon you will either have the gift of prophecy or mad cow disease.

9 When the Christians arrived in the Celt world in the 5th century the Druids had to go. The Christians had spent a couple of hundred years being thrown to the lions and that put them off bloody sacrifices for life. You'd be surprised to learn that animal sacrifices were still being made in AD 868, wouldn't you? Then you will be astounded and gobsmacked to discover that they were still being made in AD 1868. That's right, less than 150 years ago there was still a Celtic-style festival held in Cevennes in France. It involved throwing valuables and animals into a lake as offerings to the gods.

10 The Druids had some useful powers that you probably wish *you* had. They could…

- Change their shape to anything they wanted.

- Control the weather.

275

• Bring down mists to make themselves invisible.

• Travel through time.

Imagine that! There could be a Druid at your school. If your history teacher seems to know an awful lot about the Celts then maybe they *are* a Celt! A Druid on holiday in the 21st century.

Saints alive

In time the Celts dropped their gods of streams and woods and stones and became Christian. But a lot of their beliefs were carried forward into the new religion. They still had godlike humans who performed the most incredible miracles. People like Winifride and her Uncle Beuno.

Saint Gwenfrewi (or Winifride in English)

Winifride was the niece of Saint Beuno, an abbot in 6th-century Wales. Young Prince Caradoc ap Alyn loved her but she made it clear she did not want to marry him. This upset the young Prince from Wales so he drew his sword and cut off her head, as princes sometimes do when you upset them. As her head hit the ground there wasn't so much a splat! as a splash! Because a spring of water gushed out of the dry rock.

GUSH

Along came Saint Beuno, stuck her head back on her body and she was restored to life, with just a thin white line round her neck to show where she'd had her little accident. Beuno was not so kind to Caradoc. The saint cursed the Prince till the earth opened up and swallowed him. This taught him a lesson he'd never remember because he was dead before he could forget. Even his descendants suffered from Beuno's curse. They all barked like dogs until they made a pilgrimage to the well.

Winifride's well waters are now said to cure illnesses, and the well is still visited by tourists. So, don't go upsetting a prince of Wales ... unless your uncle is a saint.

Hope springs eternal

At one time heads must have been bouncing round Celtic lands like lottery numbers in a drum. Saint Llud, Saint Justinian, Saint Nectan and Saint Decuman all lost their heads and springs sprang as they fell. Saint Cadfan's shrine was set up in AD 516 and is said to cure rheumatism while Saint Canna's well water will soothe your stomach when you feel a gut ache coming on.

Saint Brigit was popular in all of the Celtic countries: Scotland, Wales, Cornwall, the Isle of Man and Brittany as well as her home in Ireland. She has so many wells it seems someone must have cut her head off and played football with it.

Brigit's crosses are still set up on farmland in Ireland to protect crops and animals. This is because she used to punish people who stole her cattle by drowning or scalding them. She didn't have Winifride's problem of princes chasing her because she made herself ugly by putting out one of her eyes.

Horrible historical joke:

Saints un-alive

The Celts became such great Christians that they practically invented many of the great Christian traditions. It's said that John Cassian was a Celt born in Scythia and he brought the first monasteries to Europe. (He pinched the idea from the Egyptians, though.) The main thing needed to be a saint is to have…

- a very good life
- a very messy death
- an incredible miracle happen.

Some Celt saints managed all three!

Saint Teilo

Saint Teilo, a 6th-century Welsh saint, is buried at a place called Llandeilo Fawr … and in Penally … and in Llandaff Cathedral. This is not very difficult if you are a saint. And, no, they didn't chop him into three and share the bits out. In one night his corpse became three bodies. Don't you wish you could do this? You could send one body to school, while one went to the seaside and the other stayed in bed and watched television.

Saint Olcan

That's Ol-can ... *not* Oil-can. Olcan's father died before he was born – the shock killed his mother who also died before he was born. She was buried and THEN Olcan was born. A passing nobleman heard baby Olcan crying, dug him up and saved his life. Don't try this in your local cemetery – body-snatching is a grave offence.

Saint Ronan

Cornish monk Saint Ronan had a pretty rough life after he was dead. His body was loaded on to a wagon and the oxen pulling it were set free. Where the wagon stopped, Ronan would be buried. But as the cart trundled along it was attacked by an angry Celt woman – people say Ronan had upset her because he took no notice when she tried to chat him up! Anyway, first she hit one of the oxen and knocked its horn off, then she hit Ronan's corpse a mighty smack in the face. He was probably glad to get safely under the ground after that!

Saint Monessa

This beautiful Irish Princess was a non-Christian Celt, but then she heard Saint Patrick preaching. She thought old Pat was wonderful and said, "Convert me to Christianity! I want to be baptized if it's the last thing I do!" Patrick baptized her ... and it was the last thing she did. She died from the happiness. (Please note: If you die from happiness while reading this book your money will not be refunded.)

286

Saint Cieran

If you're a saint it is always handy if you can work miracles after you've died. Cieran managed it. It seems that all the other saints in Ireland were praying that he'd die young. Cieran didn't let them down. He was only 33 when he died of plague in AD 548 – there were plagues even before the famous 1349 Black Death and this one got him.

Dying was a very popular thing for Cieran to do and Saint Columba cheered. But Columba took a chunk of turf from Cieran's grave and carried it with him everywhere. Years later Columba was caught in a deadly whirlpool, threw the turf in the water and the whirlpool went calm.

287

Saint Mylor

Little Mylor was only seven when his dad was murdered. The bishops persuaded the killer not to murder Mylor too. He didn't. Instead he chopped off the boy's hand and foot. Mylor hopped along to the blacksmith and had a metal hand and foot made. Miraculously his flesh-and-blood hand grew back! But Mylor's guardian cut off his head next. The boy didn't have a head-growing trick – or maybe the blacksmith didn't do heads – and he died. The murderer picked up the head happily – and dropped dead three days later.

Six dead funny facts

1 The Celts didn't mind dying too much. After all, they believed that when you left this life you woke up in the "Otherworld". The trouble is you could also die in the Otherworld … then you were reborn into this world. Then you die and go to the Otherworld, then you're reborn, then you die… (Once you've done this you will know how a yo-yo feels.)

IS THIS WORLD THE OTHER WORLD'S OTHERWORLD OR THE OTHERWORLD'S THIS WORLD?

2 The Celtic "day" began at nightfall and ended with the fading light. Similarly the year began in

November with the dying plants and sprang to life in the spring. It made sense to them to see Death as the start of your existence and Life as its end. (Well, it made sense to them, if not to you.)

3 This belief meant Celts would laugh at a funeral and cry at a birth. Christian Celts, even today, hold parties for the dead – called "wakes" – and enjoy a good laugh at a funeral.

THE DOCTOR GAVE ME THREE WEEKS TO LIVE

HOW NICE!

4 The Celts buried the dead person with some of their favourite belongings from *this* life – jewellery, weapons, clothes and, of course, food. Joints of pork seem to be the corpses' favourite food though sometimes calf, sheep and cattle bones have been found. (Personally I'd take a bag of crisps. What about you?)

I'M STILL A LITTLE PECKISH

5 They buried the very rich with a chariot. But the crafty Celts didn't waste a good chariot on a crumbling corpse. They usually buried a clapped-out chariot. Of course, the chariot needed a horse to pull it ... so the cut-throat Celts buried a clapped-out horse along with it! (Archaeologists can tell the state of the horse by the condition of its teeth and bones.)

6 One wealthy Celt was buried with 40 litres of Italian wine! Just as well the Celts didn't have breath tests or he'd be banned from driving the chariot before he even got to the afterlife!

Weird War

The Celts were fierce fighters. Some of the stories about Celt warriors are reported by the Roman historians, so they are usually believed (why *is* it that people always believe horrible historians?). In fact the Romans probably exaggerated a bit to make their own soldiers look better when they defeated the Celts.

1 Cu Chulainn became temporarily insane in battle, going into warp-spasm when he was so full of blood-lust that he couldn't tell friend from foe. This strange frenzy can still be observed on soccer pitches today!

2 The early Celt warriors fought with no clothes on except perhaps a gold band around the neck called a torque. They didn't believe in wearing armour. The Celts knew their gods would decide if they were to die that day. All the armour in the world wouldn't protect them. The Romans were protected by armour … and underpants!

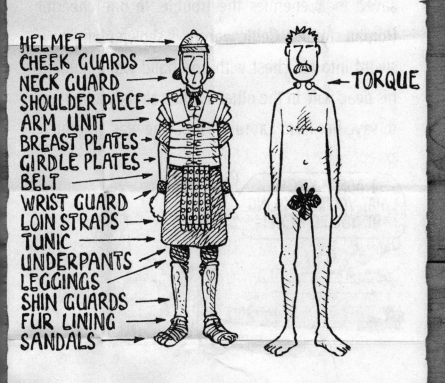

HELMET
CHEEK GUARDS
NECK GUARD
SHOULDER PIECE
ARM UNIT
BREAST PLATES
GIRDLE PLATES
BELT
WRIST GUARD
LOIN STRAPS
TUNIC
UNDERPANTS
LEGGINGS
SHIN GUARDS
FUR LINING
SANDALS

TORQUE

3 The Celts were very bad losers. If they looked like losing they killed themselves. This kind act saved their enemies the trouble. In one cheerful Roman statue a Celtic warrior is shown plunging a sword into his chest with one hand while holding his dead wife in the other. He has already killed her to save her from capture! Hope she was grateful!

I DON'T KNOW WHAT YOU'RE SMILING AT. YOU'RE NEXT!

4 The crafty Celts were great riders and invented a special saddle for fighting. They had no stirrups for their feet so there had always been a danger of the riders falling off. The Celt saddle of the 2nd and 3rd centuries BC had four high bumps (pommels is the posh word) that could be gripped with the legs. That left one hand free to guide the horse and the other to hold a weapon.

5 In AD 52 an army of 50,000 Romans defeated 250,000 Celt Gauls led by Vercingetorix. The trouble was the Celts ran wild in battle and fought as individuals. The Romans worked as a team and won.

6 The Celts liked fighting so much they didn't just fight against enemies ... they fought against each other! They also had a bit of fun fighting for other people as far away as Egypt, Greece and Asia Minor.

7 The Romans were particularly shocked by rebel British leader, Boudicca. When her husband died he left his land to Emperor Nero and his daughters. The Emperor wanted it all and had Boudicca and the daughters flogged. Big Bad Boud attacked Roman towns and was especially cruel to women prisoners. They were executed and bits of their bodies were cut off and stuck in their mouths. They then had a sharp wooden stake pushed through their bodies and they were hoisted up for everyone to see. This nasty hobby became really popular 1,400 years later when a certain Count Dracula of Romania used it against his enemies...

8 And talking about Romania … a Celt chieftain's helmet found in Ciumesti (Romania) has a large model bird perched on top. Its wings are spread and are hinged in the middle so they can flap up and down! Historians believe the chieftain would only wear it on important occasions – not in battle. It's a bit like Long John Silver having a parrot on his shoulder, only not so messy!

FLAP

FLAP
FLAP
FLAP
FLAP
FLAP

THIS IS A VERY SERIOUS OCCASION, COME BACK HERE!

☠ Cut-throat Celts

9 There is no doubt that the ancient Celts believed that the greatest prize in battle was an enemy's head. They decorated both their saddles and the doors of their houses with heads. They preserved old heads in cedar oil and brought them out every now and again to boast about them. Some boasted that they refused to part with their enemy heads even though they'd been offered the head's weight in gold.

10 The Celts believed that single combat was a good way to show off your bravery and settle an argument. Two heroes would step forward and begin by insulting each other!

Then they'd start fighting while the soldiers on both sides watched to see that they fought fairly.

Awesome Arthur

The Celts usually chose the best warrior as the leader of their tribe. If two warriors both claimed to be the best then they had to fight for the honour. One didn't have to kill the other one, just beat him in single combat.

The Celts didn't usually have fine crowns for their kings. But the winner of the battle needed some sign that he was the boss. This sign would often be a fine sword. Before the fight, the great royal sword was placed on an altar stone. The Druid presented this sword to the winner. Anyone who tried to take the new king's power from him would be cursed by the magical power of the sword.

But here's the clever bit! Some historians believe this was how a Celt called Arthur took control of the kingdom! Everybody's heard the story of Arthur and the sword IN the stone. But is the truth that Arthur fought in single combat, won, and took the sword ON the stone?

Of course, there are TWO Arthurs...

1 the warrior chief who may (or may not) have fought against the Saxon invasions of the 5th century and...

2 the King of legend who led the Knights of the Round Table into battles with dragons and giants and magic.

The trouble with Arthur 2 is that the stories always make Arthur out to be the greatest hero who ever lived.

The truth about Arthur

Over the centuries Arthur has become a British hero. Some people have built the most fantastic stories around him. They have said...

• Arthur was King of Atlantis – a kingdom that sank under the sea.

• Arthur was an alien who landed on Earth, zapped the Saxons then went off in his flying saucer.

• Arthur sailed west after his last battle and became the first European to discover America – a thousand years before Christopher Columbus.

The truth is…

1 If Arthur really existed then he lived in the "Dark Ages" when no one was writing history. A couple of monks mentioned him. Nennius said…

AT THAT TIME A GREAT NUMBER OF SAXONS WERE INVADING BRITAIN AND INCREASING. THEN ARTHUR AND THE BRITISH KINGS FOUGHT THE SAXONS. HE WAS THEIR BATTLE LEADER. THE PAGANS WERE PUT TO FLIGHT THAT DAY AND MANY OF THEM WERE SLAUGHTERED. A TWELFTH BATTLE TOOK PLACE AT MOUNT

BADON IN WHICH A SINGLE ATTACK
FROM ARTHUR KILLED 960 MEN.
NO OTHER MAN TOOK PART IN THIS
MASSACRE. IN ALL THESE BATTLES
ARTHUR WAS THE VICTOR.

2 The monk listed twelve battle sites and historians have argued about where they took place for a thousand years. No one really knows but it's fairly certain they were all over England, Wales and Scotland.

3 Historians argue over the line that says, "No other man took part in this massacre" of 960 men! Most writers agree it means no other "battle leader" took part in the massacre. If he killed 960 soldiers on his own then his little arms would be aching!

4 Arthur seems to have been the leader of some sort of travelling band of warriors. Tribal kings hired him to sort out the Saxons or pick on the Picts whenever trouble arose … but Arthur himself may not have been a king.

5 It was 600 years after his death that monks started writing histories about him and making him into the last of the Celt super-heroes.

Welsh monk, Geoffrey of Monmouth, wrote about Arthur in 1135, and added or invented or guessed at bits of Arthur's life. People believed they were "facts" because they appeared in a history book! This is an important lesson. Never believe EVERYTHING you read in a history book! Geoffrey had the date of the last battle at Camlann as AD 542, by which time Arthur would have been 100 years old! No wonder the poor old wrinkly lost!

MY LORD, THE ENEMY ATTACKS ON OUR FLANK. WHAT ARE YOU GOING TO DO?

HAVE A LITTLE LIE DOWN

6 Then, in the 1150s, poems were written based on Geoffrey's "facts" – Arthur's court at Camelot was invented in an 1180s' poem and the search for the Holy Grail was added in an 1190s' poem. Other storytellers added Merlin the magician, ladies in lakes and battles with evil knights.

7 In 1344 King Edward III of England got hold of the story and decided to have his own Knights of the Round Table. Then he changed his mind and the idea became the Knights of the Garter in 1348. Other kings of England or the United Kingdom have admired Arthur too. Henry VII named his son Arthur, Prince of Wales. But Arthur died before he came to the throne and his nasty little brother, Henry VIII, took over instead. The present Prince of Wales has Arthur as one of his middle names ... and caused such a stir with his marriage problems that some people said he should never be king. Are we doomed never to have a King Arthur? Is there a curse on the name?

8 A really large Round Table can be seen today in Winchester Castle and it is probably one of Henry III's bright ideas – it certainly isn't the real Arthur's Round Table.

9 Thomas Malory wrote a long poem called *The Death of Arthur* and it became one of the first books ever to be printed, in 1485. Arthur became a popular star and he still is today.

10 New films, books, plays, videos and magazines appear every year. There are coach trips to Arthur's sites, a King Arthur Society and you can even have a King Arthur holiday.

DORIS, WHERE'S MY KING ARTHUR SOAP?

NEAR YOUR KING ARTHUR TOOTHBRUSH, UNDER YOUR KING ARTHUR SHAVING FOAM AND THAT KING ARTHUR BATH LOTION BY YOUR KING ARTHUR FLAVOURED DENTAL FLOSS

The truth is...

- There was almost certainly a strong and successful warrior among the Celtic Britons.

- For 30 years or more he held back the flood of Saxon invaders.

- When he died the Saxons invaded the country and the Celt Britons were finished.

- We don't know the name of this last great British Celt … but we might as well call him … Arthur.

Battlefield beliefs

As well as the Roman writers there were Celt poets who told tales of daring deeds. These too became a bit exaggerated. It was many years before these stories were written down and mistakes could have been made. For example, Celt Queen Boudicca was known for many years as Boadicea because of a monk's spelling mistake!

But the stories are interesting because there could well be truth behind them. In the legend of King

Ailill Olomn's spear there are three things he mustn't do – he mustn't strike a stone, he mustn't kill a woman and he mustn't straighten the tip with his tooth. In fact, he kills a woman after she bites his ear. The spear goes through her and the tip buckles against a stone. He straightens it with his tooth ... and is cursed. He goes blind, mad and (very strangely) develops bad breath. You'd think being blind and mad, having bad breath would be the least of his worries!

315

It's a fair guess that warriors straightened spear tips with their teeth but were warned not to. The warning became a little story – rather like *Little Red Riding Hood* is a warning not to talk to strange wolves in the wood.

Here are some of the other stories that Celts went into battle believing...
1 The Celts had Battle Furies to help them in war. These war-goddesses weren't actually fighters – more, frighters. The Nemhain (Frenzy), a charming goddess, had a powerful voice (like a dinner-lady telling you to line up properly). She shrieked at the Connacht army in Ulster and a hundred soldiers dropped dead with fright.

SHE'S THEIR
SHRIEKRET
WEAPON

2 The equally delightful Macha turned into a crow during a battle and hovered over the battlefield – she

OOO! ANOTHER
HEAD LOPPED
OFF. YUM YUM!

was waiting to make a meal of the heads of the dead fighters.

3 If you saw the Badbh before a battle then it was serious bad news – she took the form of a crow, bleeding, with a rope

BLOOD STAINED
ROPES ARE OK, BUT
A RED TIE IS MORE
COMFORTABLE

around her neck. A sure sign that you are going to die. (If you see a bleeding crow before a football, hockey or netball match it is a sure sign that someone is going to lose! If the match is a draw then you clearly made a mistake – you probably saw a crow that had been supping tomato sauce.)

4 On the other hand, Badbh was sometimes seen with a man. You could hardly miss him. He had one hand, one eye and one leg – he had a roast pig on his back which was still squealing. (Well, *you'd* be squealing if you'd been roasted.) If you see the

bleeding hanged crow AND this feller hopping towards you it is probably time to get a tape measure and get measured for a coffin.

EEEEEEEEE

HOW COME NOBODY WANTS TO BE FRIENDS WITH US?

5 But be careful if you see the Morrigan. She will urge you to fight and promise that you will win … trouble is, she'll be saying exactly the same thing to the other side! Will you recognize the Morrigan? Possibly. She is red, with red hair and a red cloak, riding a chariot pulled by a red horse. In case you still don't spot her then take a close look at her horse … it only has one leg, the chariot pole passes through its body and is fastened to its head with a peg. And I forgot to mention, her mouth is on the side of her face – a useful device for people who want to lick the wax out of one ear. (If you still can't spot her then you probably need to visit your optician.)

6 The Celts were fearless fighters yet they could easily be put off a fight. They believed that there were good days for fighting and bad days. There were signs that told a warrior to fight, or to pack up and go home. If he saw a crane bird, for example, he knew that would bring him bad luck. A crane would take away your courage and your skill – three cranes would leave you with as much fight as a lettuce leaf.

I'M *DEFINITELY* NOT FIGHTING TODAY!

"DID YOU KNOW ... ?
RED WAS SAID BY THE CELTS TO BE THE COLOUR OF SOMEONE (OR SOMETHING) COMING FROM THE UNDERWORLD. (THIS IS NOT A REASON TO RUN AWAY FROM PILLAR BOXES, ROBINS OR LIVERPOOL FOOTBALL PLAYERS.)**"

How to be a hero

Celtic warriors enjoyed boasting about their victories. But they also liked to have little trophies that they could show to their friends. They were things to boast about. Here is a trophy that *you* can be proud of. To make it you will need a sharp sword, a wooden spoon and some lime (or cement).

1. Pick a fight with another hero. The more fierce he is then the greater the glory when you beat him *fig I*

2. Kill him (Please note: If he kills you then stop reading here) *see fig I*

3. Remove his head (Don't feel too bad about this, He'd do the same to you) *see fig II*

4. Remove the brain from the skull. *see fig III*

5. Mix the brain with lime to make a hard round ball

6. Show your prize at feasts and boast about your bravery

fig I

fig II

fig III

HERE'S ONE
I made
EARLIER!

This jolly little operation has its dangers – apart from the danger of your own brain ending up like a concrete football. The Celts believe that the brain can take its revenge, even after it's been removed.

Hero Conchobor killed Meisceadhra and made a trophy of his brain. But the brain was stolen and thrown at Conchobor. It hit him on the head … and stuck. For ever! In the end it drove Conchobor mad and he chopped oak trees down with his sword till he dropped dead.

IS THIS WHAT THEY CALL BRAIN DEAD?

Did you know?

The Celts did use brain power as well as muscle power sometimes. In 279 BC a Greek army broke down bridges to stop a Celt army pursuing them. The Celt land army had no boats but managed to cross the rivers by using their wooden shields as rafts. Clever Celts! Unfortunately they then went on to lose the battle, though they fought bravely – some warriors tore Greek spears out of their bodies and threw them back!

Potty prophetic hero

Place two fingers in your mouth and try speaking through them. This will not only allow you to spray your listeners with saliva, but also allow you to solve a mystery! The words you speak in this way will reveal some hidden truth.

But don't expect great things from this. The warrior Fionn used the trick to detect the death of Lomna. He came across Lomna's body and said...

HE HAS NOT BEEN KILLED BY A WILD BOAR, HE HAS NOT BEEN KILLED BY A FALL, HE HAS NOT DIED IN HIS BED!

Amazing! How did he know all these things? Not really so very amazing. Lomna's body had no head on it. Even the British police could have guessed he did "not die in his bed"!

Woe for Women

Women in history are like the managers of football teams – they send their men out to battle with the weather or with the enemy. When they win the men get all the glory – when they lose the manager gets the sack ... or the woman gets the blame. Celtic women had an equally difficult life...

- Women of the Parisii tribe (now in East Yorkshire) were around 1.58 metres in height on average and most only lived to their early twenties. Giving birth to children was very dangerous and probably killed a lot of them.

- Celt women wore make-up made from juices of berries. Eyebrows were darkened with berry juice, a herb called ruam gave a red tint to cheeks and berry juice was used to redden the lips. The women also painted their nails. But a woman had to protect her eye shadow – the men liked to use it too!

- Women were proud of their long hair and carried their combs in a special comb-bag. Hair braids have been found in Ireland that are 1.5 metres long and even a warrior like Boudicca wore her hair to her knees. But some things never change – it seemed Celt men preferred blondes. Both men and women wore golden balls plaited into the end of their hair and the men wore earrings too, as many do today. By this time you will have realized that the Celts loved their hair. The warriors bleached it with lime and arranged it into wild spikes. When a young man left home to become a warrior he had his hair cut to show that he was no longer a child.

- Large families shared a house – children lived with aunts and uncles and grandparents. Roman Julius Caesar said that groups of 10 to 12 men often shared wives. But the fact that the men shared the house doesn't mean they shared the women! No one can be sure.

- Graves have been discovered which show that some Celt women rose to become chiefs of their tribes. They were buried with battle chariots and weapons. Famous Macha of the Red Hair was said to rule all of Ireland and some historians believe she was a real person, not just a legend.

These warrior princesses were not the only women to be involved in war…

Ten things you never knew about fighting females

1 Irish landowners were expected to fight for their lord if he went to war. And if the landowner was a woman she was expected to fight. In the 6th century AD Saint Adamnan forced the law to be changed.

2 Women warriors in Irish tribes were teachers – but they didn't teach children to read and write. They trained the boys to fight. Do you know any women teachers like that?

THE TEST TOMORROW IS ON DISEMBOWELLING, SO STUDY YOUR SWORD SLASHES TONIGHT

3 Celtic women could be tribal chiefs and there was a woman army leader who led a group of Brigantian soldiers in an attack on the Romans some time between AD 71 and 83. Teuta led a Celtic tribe in the Mediterranean that took on the Greeks then the Romans. The Romans threatened to turn the whole of their army against her and sent a message warning her to behave. She had the messenger murdered! A huge Roman fleet forced her to make peace.

4 However, the more usual role of women was to spectate from carts and platforms at the back of the fighters and shout encouragement to their own fighters and insults or curses to the opposition – a bit like cheerleaders at American Football games. When the Gergovian Celts of Gaul lost to the Romans, the Celt women took all their clothes off in the hope that the Romans would spare them. Some hope!

5 Princess Canna was forced to marry Sinorix – King of the Storms – after he had murdered her husband. But it was a stormy marriage. One evening she offered Sinorix wine.

6 Women were not restricted to staying at home, teaching children, cooking or farming while the men went off to fight. Women in Gaul followed professions including wine-seller, butcher, doctor and chemist.

7 This may make women seem strong and powerful but Roman leader Julius Caesar said that in Gaul, men had the power of life or death over the women. He was probably wrong when he went on…

WHEN THE HEAD OF A NOBLE FAMILY DIES AND THERE IS SOME SUSPICION ABOUT THE DEATH, THEN HIS WIDOW IS QUESTIONED UNDER TORTURE. IF SHE IS FOUND GUILTY OF HIS DEATH THEN SHE IS SENTENCED TO BURN AND SENT TO THE FLAMES WITH THE MOST CRUEL TORMENTS.

8 It's possible that women were Druid priestesses. Tacitus described the British forces which faced Suetonius Paulinus on Anglesey...

ON THE OPPOSITE SHORE STOOD THE BRITISH ARMY WITH ITS DENSE CROWD OF ARMED WARRIORS. BETWEEN THE COLUMNS DASHED WOMEN IN BLACK GOWNS LIKE THE GODDESSES OF WAR, THEIR HAIR WILD, WAVING FLAMING TORCHES. ALL AROUND WERE THE DRUIDS, TERRIFYING OUR SOLDIERS.

These women were also involved with human sacrifices. Tacitus said the Romans found the grisly remains of blood and guts on their altars in the woods.

9 Some also had the power of seeing into the future. Diocletian was a simple soldier in the Roman Army when he was paying his bill at a tavern. A Celtic woman approached him and said...

338

Years later Diocletian killed the Emperor's leading bodyguard and became Emperor – just as the woman had predicted. The name of the Emperor's bodyguard was "Aper" ... a name meaning "Boar"!

10 You can't always trust historians, of course. A Greek geographer called Strabo lived from about 40 BC till about AD 52 and he gave a description of priestesses living on an island off the coast of France. Many historians believe this island was Britain and the people by then would have been Celts. But would you have liked to pay a visit to their church? His report goes...

Posidonius says there is an island in the ocean, not far from land. The women there honour the god Dionysus and worship him with ceremonies and sacred rituals. It is their custom, once a year, to remove the roof from their temple and cover it again the same day before sunset. Each woman must carry part of the load. But if any woman lets her load drop then she is torn to pieces by the others. They then carry the pieces of her round the temple, chanting and do not stop till the madness passes away. But it always happens that somebody pushes against a woman who is chosen to suffer this fate!

Imagine that! Being torn apart by a bunch of roofless women! Men were not allowed to land on the island. I can't imagine many men would want to!

Tall tales

And in the ancient Celtic stories naturally women are the villains. In Celt legends there are some strange women around.

1 In Irish legend Medb is cruel, jealous, unreliable and gets her power through witchcraft. In the end she was killed by the son of one of her victims. He killed her with a sling-shot like David killed Goliath ... but instead of a stone he hit her with a piece of cheese! (If it was soft cheese she'd be all right but if it was hard cheese then it was hard cheese for her.)

2 Boann made the mistake of visiting a well. Husband Nechtan was guardian of the well and told her not to go there. Nosey Boann had to have a look, didn't she? As a result the water gushed out of the well, drowned her and formed a river – now known as the Boyne in Eire. It's said she's in there somewhere. If you ever go swimming in the Boyne and find a skeleton, you'll know who it is!

3 Rhiannon was accused of murdering her baby son. In fact he was pinched by an evil spirit but Rhiannon got the blame. Her ladies-in-waiting killed a puppy and smeared Rhiannon with blood as she slept. When she woke, covered in blood with no baby, her husband believed she had got rid of the baby's body ... by eating it!

4 A girl, Etain, was turned into a fly by a jealous goddess. This was quite useful because she could hum the god Midhir to sleep with her buzzing – or wake him up when danger came near. The jealous goddess was not satisfied and chased her so long and hard that Etain buzzed her way into a woman's wine glass. The woman drank the wine and swallowed Etain. (And before you ask, no, the woman did NOT swallow a spider to catch the fly, or swallow a bird to catch the spider that wriggled and wriggled and tickled inside her. That's another story altogether.) So anyway, next time you feel like swatting a fly, remember ... it could be some poor cursed girl!

True tale of terror

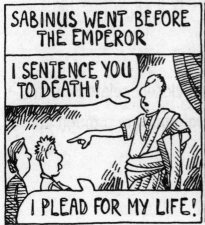

Eponina's wish had been to go to the Otherworld with her husband. She got her wish and they were executed that very day. Brave Celtic woman? Or a waste of a good life? What would you have done?

Cut-throat women

Some German tribes were closely related to the Celts. The Cimbrian holy women were a tough and bloodthirsty lot...

THEY WERE GREY WITH AGE, WORE WHITE TUNICS AND, OVER THESE, CLOAKS OF THE FINEST LINEN AND BRONZE GIRDLES. THEY WERE BAREFOOT. THESE WOMEN WOULD ENTER THE CAMP OF THEIR WARRIORS, SWORD IN HAND, AND GO UP TO THE PRISONERS. THEY WOULD THEN CROWN THEM AND LEAD THEM UP TO A LARGE BRONZE VESSEL. ONE OF THEM WOULD MOUNT A STEP

AND, LEANING OVER THE CAULDRON, CUT THE THROAT OF A PRISONER WHO WAS HELD UP OVER THE VESSEL'S RIM. OTHERS CUT THE BODY OPEN AND, AFTER INSPECTING THE ENTRAILS, WOULD FORETELL VICTORY FOR THEIR COUNTRYMEN.

You'll notice the women do not foretell the "result" … they foretell the "victory". In other words they know what the entrails (or guts) will say before they kill their victim! Seems like a waste of a good prisoner to be honest.

This story was told by Greek geographer Strabo and may have had some truth in it. However, do NOT try this at home. It makes a terrible mess on

348

the carpet. If you want to look into the future then read your horoscope in the daily paper.

Cut-throat corpses

Women were also the victims of cut-throat carvers. In late Roman Britain there were many examples of people being buried with their heads removed and placed between their legs. Most of these were middle-aged or elderly women.

It's hard to say if they were beheaded before or after they were dead, but they were all beheaded very cleanly at the same neck bone and from the front. But why?

Some historians think it was so the women could see their way into the next life – a pair of eyes at your feet can come in very handy sometimes!

Or it could have been a punishment for witchcraft

– many of these bodies have their jaws removed. That should shut them up in the next life all right.

Some women's heads are buried in wells – one in an Oxfordshire village called Headington (honest!).

❝DID YOU KNOW...?
FROM THE ANCIENT LAWS OF HYWEL DDA WE KNOW THAT MEDIEVAL WELSH KINGS HAD A SERVANT KNOWN AS A "FOOT HOLDER". BELIEVE IT OR NOT THE FOOT HOLDER HELD THE KING'S FEET! FROM THE TIME THE KING SAT DOWN TO EAT HIS EVENING MEAL, THE FOOT HOLDER

TOOK THE KING'S FEET IN HIS LAP AND HELD THEM TILL HE WENT TO BED. WHILE THE KING'S FEET WERE OFF HIS KINGDOM HE COULD RELAX – HE WASN'T KING FOR A WHILE. THE FOOT HOLDER HAD THE POWER; CRIMINALS COULD ASK THE FOOT HOLDER FOR A PARDON AND HE WOULD PROBABLY ALLOW THEM TO GO FREE – THE KING WOULD HAVE HAD TO PUNISH THEM. **"**

Crazy Celt Life

The Celts were farmers – when they weren't hunting animals or fighting Romans. They kept cows and sheep and hens and so on. Sounds idyllic, doesn't it? But would you like to have lived as a Celt? Read the facts and make up your own mind…

1 The Celts dressed to keep warm but they also liked to put on a bit of a show. Women wore checked skirts and when they went to important meetings they wore make-up, bracelets, anklets, necklaces, finger-rings, earrings and hairpins. Richer women also wore the gold neck bands (torques) that were worn by hero warriors. The Celts had no buttons – they used pins or brooches and those pins would be decorated too. Imagine having decorations on your zips!

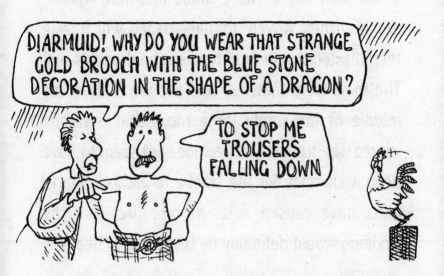

DIARMUID! WHY DO YOU WEAR THAT STRANGE GOLD BROOCH WITH THE BLUE STONE DECORATION IN THE SHAPE OF A DRAGON?

TO STOP ME TROUSERS FALLING DOWN

2 Irish Celts seem to have been very clean people. They washed hands and feet every morning and had a full bath every night. They scrubbed themselves with soap and a linen cloth. The good news is that the water was usually heated. The bad news is you'd probably share that water with the rest of the family.

3 The Celt houses were made of wattle walls — thin branches "woven" to make panels which were then plastered with mud to keep the draughts out. The roofs were thatched and the fire built in the middle of the single large room that everyone shared. The trouble is there does not seem to have been a chimney for the smoke to escape. Sparks must have caused a lot of roof fires and the smoking would definitely be bad for your health!

WHAT A GRUBBY FAMILY I BET THEY HAVEN'T HAD A BATH FOR WEEKS

DISGUSTING

4 The Celts built these houses in groups – often on the top of a hill and often with a defence wall around them. You'd call it a hill fort or a village, because you are sensible. But a horrible historian show-off would call it an "oppidum". You do not really need to know this ... but if you ever get bored on a car journey then, every time you pass a village, you can sing, "Oppidum, oppidum, oppidum-dum-dum!" till everyone in the car is driven mad.

5 Clean fingernails were a must. If someone damaged your fingernail they had to pay you for the damage under Irish law. A great Irish insult was to call a man "Ragged nails!"

6 They probably used iron bars as a sort of money. They'd swap the 80-cm bars for other goods.

Anyone with a dirty great magnet could have made a fortune as a pick-pocket!

7 The Celts had another useful type of money. You didn't have to carry it round with you … it walked! It was called a slave. These slaves could be people captured in battle or defeated during an invasion. The Romans used slaves and made wine – the Celts enjoyed wine but lived too far north to grow grapes. So the Celts swapped slaves for wine. WARNING: Do not let your parents know this or they may take you to the local off-licence and try to trade you for a can of lager.

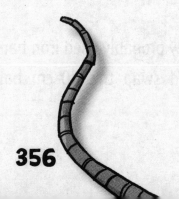

8 The Celts ate off plates made of pottery, but sometimes the plates were made of wood...

THIS FOOD TASTES BURNT

NO. THE PLATE'S MADE OF ASH

The Celts ate with their fingers, and a fussy Roman wrote...

THEY EAT CLEANLY BUT LIKE LIONS, RAISING UP WHOLE LIMBS WITH BOTH HANDS AND BITING OFF THE MEAT.

CHOMP CHOMP

9 Celts had very little furniture so they slept on the floor wrapped in animal skins — bearskin or wolfskin kept you warm. Of course, you could end up even warmer running away from the bears and wolves as you tried to nick their skins!

10 The Celts were very fond of hunting. It got rid of pests (like deer that ate their crops), provided them with food (like wild boar) and clothing (wolfskin) but above all it gave them a popular form of entertainment. They used long-handled spears, bows and metal-tipped arrows or sling shots. These weapons need a lot of practice. If you don't believe me then make one and pop off to your nearest forest. I'll bet you don't kill a single wolf or bear if you hunt all year. (No going to a zoo to win this bet! Zoos is cheating!)

WE'RE BRAVE CELT HUNTERS WAITING DEEP IN THE WILD WOODS, SOON WE WILL KILL!

YEAH, MUM DIDN'T NEED TO BRING US OUT THESE SANDWICHES

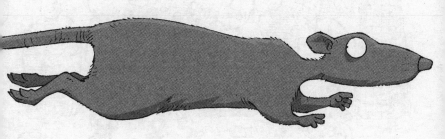

Live like a Celt

If you hopped into a time machine and were dropped in a Celt settlement then would you survive? Try this quick quiz. Get all the questions right and you'll fit in well with the Celts. Get one wrong and they may suspect you are not one of them. You'll end up with something at your throat – if you're lucky it may be a slave chain – if you're unlucky it may be a Druid's sacrificial knife!

1 The Celts loved a good party. The wine or beer is passed around. As a special guest you can drink first. But how should you drink the wine?

a) Empty your goblet in one swallow.

b) Refuse the drink until the chief has drunk first. (You could say, "Thanks but I'd rather have a Coke.")

c) Drink a small sip then pass the goblet on.

HE CAN OUTFIT US TOO...HE'S OUR TAILOR

2 As the party goes on a warrior stands up and tells everyone how he bravely fought against ten Roman soldiers and beat all of them. Everyone looks at you. What do you say?

a) "Liar! Liar! Pants on fire."

b) "You are a brave and noble warrior. I believe you and praise your courage."

c) "That's nothing, mate. I beat 20 Roman soldiers; I had one hand tied behind my back, I was wearing a blindfold and the only weapon I had was a sharp fingernail."

362

3 A wild boar has been roasted for the party. You are offered a trotter to chew on. What do you say?

a) "Thank you, that is extremely kind of you."

b) "I hope you've checked this boar for mad pig disease! Anyway, I'm a vegetarian and I'd prefer a nut cutlet."

c) "I will eat nothing but the best meat. Give me the finest flesh or you will die and I'll be roasting you on the fire."

4 The tribe explains that this is the feast of Beltane. A ceremony is about to take place. Two large bonfires are lit. The warriors ask if you know what happens next. What do you say?

a) "I guess we pop Guy Fawkes on top of one fire then set off the fireworks!"

b) "We take it in turns to plunge a hand into the fire to show our courage."

c) "We drive the cattle between the two fires and this will protect them from disease."

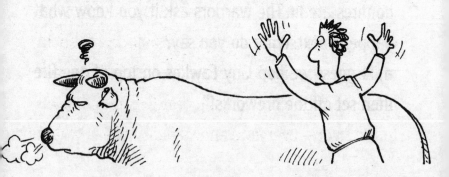

5 The Druid is a kind old bloke in a long, hooded robe. He says he has a special drink for a noble guest like you. It is made from the juice of the mistletoe. What do you do?

a) Drink it.

b) Offer to share it with the Druid.

c) Refuse to drink it. Make some excuse, like you were always taught to "Say NO to a stranger…" and they don't come much stranger than the Druid!

6 The Druid suggests that it would be good to make an offering to the goddess, Sulis. She will bless the tribe in the coming battles. You go down to the river – everyone knows Sulis lives in water.

You are given a fine knife with a gold pattern on the handle. What should you do with it?

a) Cut your hand and let a little blood drip into the river.

b) Throw the knife into the river as a rich gift.

c) Throw the knife into the river – but break it first so Sulis doesn't cut herself.

ANSWERS

All "**c)**" answers are correct. If you have just one "**a)**" or "**b)**" you would not fit in with the Celt ways and probably not survive, either. That could be your ticket to the Otherworld! Here's why…

1 The Celts drank small sips … but drank an awful lot of those small sips until they were very drunk!

2 Warriors took part in Boasting Contests. No one ever called anyone a liar but a lot of exaggerating went on and that was all part of the enjoyment.

3 The bravest warriors expected the best meat. Only a wimp would make do with less. Being given a bone is an insult – accept it and you're a wimp. Start a fight if necessary to get the best.

4 Cattle were kept inside the village fence all winter. At the beginning of May they were driven out on to the grass meadows for summer grazing. The fires represented the warming and life-giving sun and the Druids drove the cattle between two fires to protect them from evil. Other big days included 1 February, known as Imbolc – the start of the lambing season – plenty of ewes milk for cheese. 31 July was Lughnasadh, when crops were ripening and a party for the gods would make sure they were safely gathered in.

5 A Roman historian called Pliny said, "The Celts believe that the mistletoe, taken in a drink, is a cure for all poisons." But the truth is that Druids must have known that mistletoe is in fact a poison – they gave it to sacrificial victims. Maybe it knocked them unconscious so they wouldn't struggle so much when the Druids cut their throats!

6 The Celts always broke or bent a knife before offering it to Sulis. They also threw their most valuable possessions into the rivers, including solid gold cups. But if Sulis lived in water, what would she want with a cup?

DID YOU KNOW?

The Celts grew grain and when they had spent all year growing the stuff they put most of it in a hole in the ground. This is not because they were crazy Celts, but because a hole in the ground would keep it fresh until they were ready to grind it into flour.

Flour was made by placing grain on a large flat stone called a quern – then rubbing a stone over the grain. It took 90 minutes to make a kilo of flour. After the 2nd century BC a rotary quern was invented and a kilo of flour took just 10 minutes to produce.

The grain pits were also used to dump dog or horse sacrifices. Imagine opening your flour bag from the supermarket and finding a bit of dead dog. You'd probably never eat bread again!

If you want a taste of Celtic life then try these recipes...

Pease pudding

You need:

250g dried green peas
pinch of mint herb
pinch of thyme herb
25g butter
half a teaspoonful of salt

Method:

1 Soak the dried peas for 12 hours (overnight is best).

2 Put the peas and the herbs in a saucepan and boil them in half a litre of water for half an hour. They should be soft and the skins loose.

3 Pour them into a sieve to let the water drain away, then use a spoon to force the peas through the sieve, giving a pea paste. (If you're really lazy then use a blender. Celts did not have blenders.)

4 Stir in the butter and salt then place the mixture in a greased pudding basin. Cover it with foil (which the Celts didn't have) and put the basin in a covered pan of boiling water. Boil it for an hour, but don't let it boil dry. WARNING: Puddings boiled in this way have a nasty habit of giving the cook third-degree burns. Get an adult to do this for you (so they get the burns, while you get to eat the pudding).

5 Take the foil off the basin, put a plate over the top

and turn the plate and the basin upside down. If you're lucky the pease pudding will come out in a neat, basin-shaped lump. (If you're unlucky it will come out as a slimy green mess, but eat it anyway.)

Porridge

You need:

50g oatmeal
600ml water
pinch of salt
milk

Method:

1 Boil the water in a saucepan and add the salt.
2 Sprinkle in the oatmeal a little at a time and stir each time you add some.
3 Boil for 20 minutes.
4 Serve in bowls and stir in some milk.
5 If you prefer it sweet then stir in a spoonful of honey – the Celts didn't have sugar.

(This may taste quite pleasant, but most Celts ate it every day and you could soon become sick of it!)

Awesome animals

It was a hard life being a Celt, dodging the Druids and running from the Romans. But it was worse for the animals. The Celts were very close to nature and they told remarkable tales about animals. They also had some strange beliefs about them. Believe these stories if you want...

Deer

• Cernunnos was Lord of All the Stags and appeared as a man with antlers. It is very useful to walk around with a coat rack on your head but it's murder when you want to wash your hair in the sink.

- Irish Prince Tathan landed in Wales to set up a monastery. As his crew threw a rope to the shore a stag stepped forward and put a hoof on the rope to prevent the ship drifting away. Tathan went off to teach the wild Welsh about Christianity.

- When Tathan and his friends returned to the ship they were weak from hunger. Nobody had so much as a bag of crisps (well, they hadn't been invented, had they?). But the stag came to the rescue yet again. "Eat me," he said. So they did. Stag steak is very tasty they reckon, especially with mushy peas and chips.

Pigs

The Celts believed
that pigs (and sows
in particular) were

very wise. It made sense to listen to what a pig had
to say. There are lots of tales about swine-herds
who turn out to be princes in disguise. If you
wanted to get a head, get a pig.

- St Brannoc set up a church where he found
  a sow with her piglets – a dream told him to
  do this.

- A boar appears on many Celtic coins (where now
  we have the queen's head – no comments please
  about bores or pigs or you could end up in the
  Tower of London).

376

• The Goddess of Hunting, Archinna, is usually pictured riding a boar with a dagger in her hand. She is clearly into pork chops.

Wrens

• The Celts told a story about a competition for the king of the birds. The eagle flew highest and claimed to be king. But a wren had hitched a ride on the eagle's back and flew still higher. The wren was king of the birds.

• Wrens had a tough time at New Year. They were killed because the Celts believed that it was a way of saying goodbye to the old year and bringing luck to the new. It was not, of course, very lucky for a wren.

• Until recently sailors still believed that the feather of a wren protected them from drowning, especially if the wren was killed on New Year's Day. This led to the mass slaughter of wrens in the old Celt kingdom, the Isle of Man, because the sailors' protection only lasted one year.

Dogs

• Dogs were respected in Celtic life. They were useful for hunting, and they also protected their owners.

• The lick of a dog was supposed to heal a wound. WARNING: Never, ever, try this even if your dog has just gargled with antiseptic!

• The God of the Underworld had a pack of white dogs with red ears. If you ever see such a dog you can tell it to go to Hell, because that's just telling it to go home!

• Druids may have respected dogs but this didn't stop them from chewing dog flesh for mystic power.

Miserable medicine

• Celt doctors bored into a patient's skull to relieve pressure on the brain. This was particularly useful if your skull had been bashed in battle.

• The Celts also believed in the healing powers of water. The Romans are famous for their healing waters at England's west-country city of Bath. But the Celts discovered it before the Romans got

379

there and were using the waters long after the Romans had gone. The waters probably helped with some illnesses but the Celts believed it was the Goddess, Sulis, who really healed them.

- The Romans taught the Celts the trick of writing your problem on a thin piece of lead, rolling it up and dropping it into the water. (This is a bit like taking a prescription from the doctor and giving it to the chemist. The difference is we can read the lead inscriptions even today – the handwriting of doctors is impossible to read!) No one worried if they couldn't write. They simply made a little model of their poorly parts and dropped it in the water!

- While you were at the Bath waters – drinking it and bathing in it – there were doctors hanging around who offered to cure you if the waters didn't work. And, while you were there, you could also take the time to curse somebody who had upset you. A lot of curse messages have been found. They said things like...

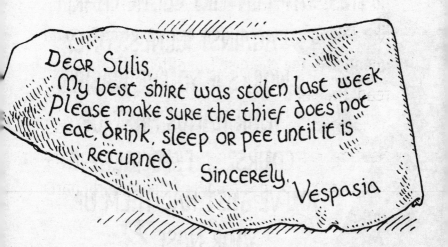

Dear Sulis,
My best shirt was stolen last week
Please make sure the thief does not
eat, drink, sleep or pee until it is
returned.
                Sincerely,
                        Vespasia

"DID YOU KNOW ... ?
TO PROTECT YOURSELF AGAINST
ILLNESS YOU SHOULD TAKE YOUR
MIDDLE TWO FINGERS, PLACE THEM
IN YOUR MOUTH AND SPREAD THEM.
THIS 9TH–CENTURY CELTIC CHARM
AGAINST ILLNESS ONLY
WORKS IF YOU'VE WASHED
YOUR HANDS FIRST, OF
COURSE ... ESPECIALLY IF
YOU'VE JUST HAD THEM UP
YOUR NOSE. **"**

382

CELTIC LIFE — TEST YOUR TEACHER

1 What did the Celts put on their ponies to protect them during races?

a) Shin guards (like footballers wear) made of whale bones.

b) Crash-helmets made of metal.

c) Leather boots cushioned with sheepskin.

2 How did Bronze-Age Scots try to strengthen their fortress walls to keep the Celts out?
a) They cemented the stones together.
b) They nailed the stones together.
c) They set huge bonfires against the wall to melt the stones together.

3 Some Celts got away with a debt in a curious way. What did they say to someone they owed money to?
a) "I'll pay you in the next life."
b) "I'll toss a coin with you — double or quits."

c) "You can have my wife instead of the money."

4 The Pict tribes of Scotland knew about it, but modern Brits only found it in 1933. What?

a) Celtic football team.

b) Invisible ink.

c) The Loch Ness Monster.

385

5 St Cybi was a brilliant child. A writer said this incredible child could do what at the age of just seven years?

a) Read a book.

b) Sacrifice a goat.

c) Learn the Bible and recite it from memory.

6 Skeletons of Celt women have been found buried with their rings. But where were they wearing them?

a) On their fingers.

b) On their toes.

c) In their noses.

7 When the Celts became Christian you could still spot the difference between their monks and the Roman monks. How?

a) They wore blue robes dyed in woad.

b) They shaved their heads from ear to ear, not in a neat circle.

c) They chanted their songs in the Gaelic language, not Latin.

8 Where did the Picts get their
name from?

a) They were the chosen people
of the gods —
the Picked or
Pict.

b) The first
iron tools
they made were
stone-breakers called "Picks".

c) The Romans thought they were
like "Pictures" because they
painted themselves.

9 If you killed a child under
the age of seven, what would be
your punishment?

a) You would be fined three cows.

b) You would be hanged.

c) You would have the hand that did the killing cut off.

10 Historians argue about exactly who King Arthur was. One thing's for certain. Arthur was not his proper name — just a nickname. What does "Arthur" mean?

a) He who fights on two sides.

b) Great leader of 100 battles.

c) Bear.

WHO CALLED ME TEDDY?

☠ Cut-throat Celts

ANSWERS

1 b) Pony caps, with holes for the ears, have been found at Celtic sites in the Shetlands. But what on earth were they doing to need this sort of head protector? Pony-American-Football?

2 c) The Bronze-Age Celts of Scotland created these "vitrified forts" where the stones were heated till they were "welded" together. One can be seen at Craig Phadrig near Inverness. Don't try this on your house – bricks don't melt.

3 a) This worked for Celts who believed they were getting a good deal if they could collect money in the Otherworld. If you really want to persuade someone that you can be trusted then take the Celtic Curse:

If I break my promise may the skies fall upon me, may the seas drown me and may the earth rise up and swallow me!

However, the bad news is that modern Celt shopkeepers don't believe this line and will not give you a bar of chocolate or a mountain bike if you promise to pay in the next life. Sorry.

4 c) The Picts carved pictures on stones, and one stone stands at Aberlemno village between Forfar and Brechin. It shows a long-nosed swimming creature like an elephant – except its trunk comes from between its ears. This ties in with the Celtic legend of St Columba (AD 521–597) who tamed such a monster in Loch Ness. Another monk was less lucky – he let the lake monster plough his field for him. When the job was finished the monster vanished ... taking the monk with him!

NOW THERE'S SOMETHING YOU DON'T SEE EVERY DAY

5 a) Cybi could read. This might not amaze you as much as it amazed the monk who wrote his life story, but being able to read was very rare in the 6th century. If you can read this then you probably could read at seven. Why not go home and tell your parents, "Did you know I could be a saint? I really think that means you should double my pocket money."

6 b) There wouldn't have been much point in wearing a ring under your shoes – no one would see your jewellery and it would be uncomfortable. No Celtic shoes have ever been found so the toe-rings suggest that women often wore sandals.

7 b) They shaved their heads from ear to ear but sometimes the Celt monks left a tuft of hair at the top of the head. A Saxon monk called Bede (who shaved a round bald patch) thought they looked a bit ridiculous. Maybe he should have looked in a mirror! Some historians think the Celt monks may have copied the Druids in this hair fashion. Celt monks also amazed the Europeans by wearing black eye make-up – a fashion they kept from Celt warriors.

8 c) The Picts were nicknamed "Picture People" by the Romans but their real name was Cruitne. The Picts lived in Scotland where they were joined by the Scots who came from Ireland. In time there were more Scots than Picts so Pictland became Scotland. Got it? It could be worse – the Britons called them Priteni. Edinburgh could now be the capital of Priteniland. Try spelling that in a geography lesson some wet Wednesday.

9 a) A child under seven was considered to be worth as much as a priest! Any child under 14 could not commit a crime – the parents had to take the blame. This hasn't changed much 2,000 years later. If you skip school then your parents end up with a fine.

10 c) 'Arthur' meant "Bear". The other two nicknames are from the Dark, or Middle, Ages. Celt leader Vercingetorix meant "Great leader of 100 battles" while a leader in Gaul was named Ambigatus meaning "He who fights on two sides" ... which is a funny thing to do. If he was fighting on both sides he'd have to try to kill himself while at the same time try to stop himself being killed by himself. He could end up in more knots than a boy scout's tent-rope.

Cheerless children

You think school is bad? You'd probably prefer it to being a Celtic child. All work and very little play. From the time you could walk you'd be given jobs like weeding the fields, combing the wool ... and watching the fleas and lice jump out on to you as you comb. (That should keep you up to scratch!)

AH, A COUPLE OF YOUNG BLOODS

Sets of coloured glass counters, a little like modern marbles, have been found at Celtic sites. They seem to be from some board game a bit like Ludo. Unfortunately the Celts were not great writers so there's no rule book with the counters and no one knows how the game was played.

397

💀 Cut-throat Celts

Simple games *have* survived from the period and here's one you can try...

Knife-cloth-stone

You'll need:

• two players, preferably with at least one hand each.

All you do is:

1 On the count of three each player brings a hand out from behind their back. They have made a shape with that hand.

• A pointing finger is a knife.

• A spread hand is a cloth.

• A tight fist is a stone.

2 The winner is the one whose object can destroy the other player's. So…

• A knife beats a cloth because it can cut it.

• A stone beats a knife because it can blunt it.

• A cloth beats a stone because it can wrap around it.

3 A point is scored every time a player wins. The first to score 10 is the winner.

Hurley

The Irish have a rough form of hockey known to the Celts as "hurley", and in modern Irish as "hurling". You'll need:

- two teams of 15 players each with a hurling stick – like a hockey stick with a broad end
- two goals (like five-a-side soccer goals with extended uprights to make an "H" shape)
- a hard ball like a rounders ball.

ARE WE WINNING?

WE'RE JUST A HEAD

All you do is:

1 The aim is to score a "Goal" – three points if it goes under the crossbar, one point over the crossbar but between the posts.

2 Play like hockey – except you can carry the ball on the hurling stick for as far as you want and you can catch the ball in the hand, but…

WHAP!

A HOLE IN ONE

3 You can't pick up the ball from the ground in the hand, throw the ball or run with it in the hand more than two strides.

4 Horrible hurling: you are not allowed to use your stick to batter or trip an opponent … but ancient warriors are said to have played this game with the head of an enemy. WARNING: Any player trying to play with a head today will be banned for one game (and probably locked up for life). Referees do not accept the excuse, "But the cut-throat Celts did it."

Baile

This game is a bit like team-golf.

You'll need:

• four or more players, each with a hockey stick and a ball

- a hole in the ground about a metre wide. (This may be difficult to dig in your school playground. A chalk circle may have to do!)

All you do is:

1 The aim is to hit the hole (or target circle) with a ball.

2 One player is the goalkeeper. He or she plays against the rest.

3 The team form a line facing the hole, at least 10 metres away. (This can be altered to more, or less, as you learn the game and want to make it more even.)

4 Team players strike a ball, one at a time, and try to hit the target. The goalkeeper tries to stop a ball hitting the target.

5 When everyone on the team has had a shot at the target then the score is counted – one point for a hit.

6 The team then defends the target while the goalkeeper takes a shot with each ball and tries to score more than the team.

Note 1: A Celt story describes one boy playing in goal against 150 – he stopped every ball. When it was his turn to shoot he scored with every one of his 150 shots! As a modern hockey player he would be wanted by every team in the world!

Note 2: Pottery images of this game show that the players wore no clothes. You could try this if you wanted but you might be arrested by the police, who are not trained to understand Celtic laws.

Note 3: The images also appear to show the game being played with a head instead of a ball. You probably wouldn't want to use a head in your school yard because heads don't bounce as well as tennis balls. They just sort of hit the ground and go "splat!"

I WAS TALKING IN CLASS SO MISS SMITH SAID I HAD TO GO SEE THE HEAD

DID YOU KNOW?

- Boys and girls in Celt Ireland were sent away from home as soon as they were old enough — probably about seven. They went to live with a family in a neighbouring tribe. This taught them they belonged to the whole tribe and not just one father and mother. They stayed there until they were about 17 years old.

- The boys were not taught how to fight by the tribe's champion – he'd be far too busy. Instead they were often taught by women warriors.
- Girls married at the age of 12 to 14 and until then would be said to be "beside her father's plate".

Crime and Punishment

The Celts may have seemed wild and lawless to the Romans but in fact they had their own type of law and order. The Druids took on special jobs. Some advised the people or the king, some acted as priests, some as fortune-tellers and some as judges. The judge-Druids were known as Brehons.

A Brehon settled arguments, listened to complaints and decided if there was a crime. The Brehon could also order punishments if he or she thought someone was guilty.

Trial by the gods

The Brehons could not always be sure of someone's guilt. There were no video surveillance cameras, no fingerprints, no blood tests and none of the scientific tests that today's police have. But the Brehons believed they had something better. A god who has seen everything!

All they had to do was leave the decision to chance – the god would make sure that chance pointed out the right victim. Why not try it and see if it works?

Casting the woods

This system was used by Druids in murder trials ... but we don't really want to murder someone just to test it ... no, not even the class bully deserves that.

You'll need:

- three people – one Brehon Judge, two suspects
- three pieces of wood – sticks

410

from ice lollies would be perfect. (Yes, I know the Celts didn't have ice lollies – stop trying to be so clever and just get on with the trial, will you?) You will also need something to scratch words on to the sticks and a bag or hat to hide the sticks in.

All you do is:

1 Place a valuable object on a table – a watch, a jelly baby, the crown jewels … anything.

2 The Brehon turns his or her back.

3 One of the suspects steals the valuable object and hides it on their person.

4 The Brehon then holds the "casting-the-woods" trial…

- If the Celt farmers discovered someone's animal had damaged a fence then who had the job of fixing the fence? The animal's owner, since cattle aren't very handy with a hammer. How will they decide whose beast did the damage? By casting the woods.

- And if a Celt accidentally hurt a bee then he had to pay the owner of the hive for the loss. Everyone had bees and hives. How did they know which hive the bee came from? No, they didn't have little rings around their bees' knees like pigeons. The Celts would cast the woods.

Why can't we just do this today? Two cars crash – who's to blame? Cast the woods! Two soccer teams are level after extra time in a cup match. Who goes on to the next round? Cast the woods! You need £5 to go to the cinema. Who should pay? Cast the woods — just make sure each wood has the letters D-A-D scratched on it!

"DID YOU KNOW ... ?
SOMETIMES A DRUID JUDGE
DECIDED THAT A WHOLE FAMILY
WAS TO BLAME FOR THE CRIME
OF ONE PERSON. THIS WOULD BE
A BIT LIKE YOUR BROTHER
BREAKING A WINDOW ... BUT THE
COST OF REPAIRING IT IS TAKEN
FROM YOUR POCKET MONEY!"

Make the punishment fit the crime

Here are five Celt crimes … if you were a judge, what would *you* do to the criminal found guilty?

CRIME

1 Deserting your tribe in battle

2 Calling a woman ugly

3 killing a woman who has run off with your husband

4 Burning a building down

5 Violent crime

Punishment

A Fined

B Exile

C Hanged from a tree

D Death by drowning

E no punishment

ANSWERS

1 c) Traitors and deserters were hanged from trees. Trees were particularly important to Celts because they were like a picture of life – roots in the underworld and branches in this world. Hanging sent a man straight to the Otherworld!

2 a) You were fined for insulting a woman's appearance, making up a nickname for them, making fun of some weakness they had or for telling an untrue story about them.

3 e) A woman who killed her husband's girlfriend could get her revenge in any way she wanted … so long as she did it within three days of finding out about them. After three days she should have calmed down – any action then becomes a crime.

I CAN STOP RUNNING ON TUESDAY

4 b) Celts believed that their land went as far as the ninth wave from the shore. Exiled criminals were set adrift with no oars or sail or steering paddle. They were given just a knife and some fresh water and left to the mercy of the gods. They usually died, but if they were swept back to the shore they became a slave. In legends there were saints and heroes who survived this punishment and went on to do great deeds. In the real world it was a harsh sentence often given to women who murdered or anyone who broke into a Christian Celt church.

5 d) Vicious criminals were sometimes drowned in swamps under a cover of wattle hurdles but this practice probably died out in the AD years. Drowning by trampling in a swamp also seems to have been a punishment for cowards and shirkers who left others to do all the work. So, next time your dad asks you to help with the washing up, make sure he's not a Celt before you refuse!

❝ DID YOU KNOW ... ? THE CELTS HAD A LAW AGAINST DAMAGING TREES. BUT YOUR PUNISHMENT DEPENDED ON WHAT SORT OF TREE IT WAS! YOU WERE IN DEEP TROUBLE IF YOU HARMED AN OAK, APPLE, ASH, HAZEL, YEW OR FIR TREE. IT WAS LESS SERIOUS IF YOU DAMAGED AN ALDER, WILLOW, BIRCH OR ELM. **❞**

Weird Words

The Celts couldn't write because their religious leaders wouldn't let them. Those Druids believed that the written word meant power. They kept calendars (with a month counted off each time the moon appeared) and marked off what days were good for things like invading Rome or sacrificing a cow.

Eventually the Celts made an alphabet similar to the Vikings. It was made up of straight lines because these letters were carved on to stone or wood. Historians have been able to learn something of Celt life from these carvings. The Welsh alphabet had 30 letters and looked like this:

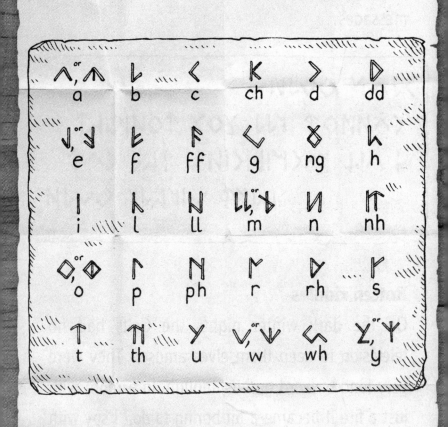

421

Being able to write is very useful. You can leave messages…

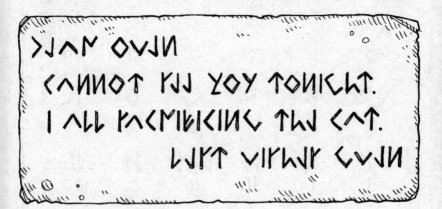

Rotten riddles

On the dark winter nights the Celts had no television to keep themselves amused. They were very fond of word games, though. In a room with just a fire it became a bit boring to do, "I spy with my little eye something beginning with F."

422

DON'T TELL ME, LET ME GUESS, COULD IT POSSIBLY BE PERHAPS, THAT YELLOWY FLICKERING HOT THINGY

So the Celts had a good line in riddles – puzzles to which you had to guess the answer. Could *you* be a Celt Clever Clogs and solve this one…?

In come two legs carrying one leg,
Lay down one leg on three legs,
Out go two legs, in come four legs,
Out go five legs, in come two legs,
Snatches up three legs, flings it at four legs
And brings back one leg.

The awful thing about riddles is that the answer is so easy once it's explained! The longer you think about it the more satisfying it is to get the answer in the end. So, DO NOT read the answer for 24 hours! Go and read something else ... the *Bible*, the *Encyclopaedia Britannica*, your sister's diary – anything.

ANSWER

Well? Did you guess it? If not, did you spend 24 hours trying? No? You should be ashamed of yourself. Here's the answer ... A woman (two legs) comes in carrying a leg of lamb (one leg) and puts it down on a stool (three legs). In comes a dog (four legs) and runs off with it. Now, even you can work out the ending from there!

Celtic compass

The Celts were skilful sailors and needed a good sense of direction. After all, they didn't want to sail over the edge of the world which (as we can all see) is flat. But the Celtic sailors didn't describe directions as North, South, East or West. They used colours. The sun rose in the "purple" and by midday was in the "white". You too could become a geographical genius by learning this chart…

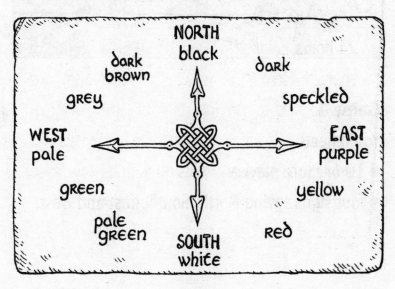

💀 **Cut-throat Celts**

Celt compass games

Of course simply learning these directions is no fun. You have to use them. Try giving someone directions using the Celtic compass…

HOW WAS I TO KNOW HE WAS COLOUR BLIND?

Game 1

You'll need:

- 10 or more players
- four signs saying North, South, East and West.

All you do is:

1 Place the cards on each of the four walls of a large room or hall.

2 There is one "caller" and the rest are runners.

3 The caller selects a colour – say, "white" – and shouts it.

4 The players have to run to the correct sign – in this case "South".

SHARON'S ALWAYS BEEN VERY COMPETITIVE AT GAMES

5 The last one to touch the south wall is out.

6 The game continues with one player dropping out each round. Obviously, the corners are the colours or shades between the main compass points. "Dark" or "Speckled" means north-east.

7 The winner is the last player in. Change callers and start again.

8 When the players are getting faster then add a new call … "Cut-throat!" This means "freeze". Everyone who moves after the call is out.

Game 2

You'll need:

- at least two players
- a room full of obstructions (like chairs)
- a scarf for a blindfold.

All you do is:

1 The aim is for the leader to get the blindfolded partner safely across the room to a target without bumping, breaking or even touching an obstruction in between. (It would also be nice if the blindfolded partner does not break a leg.)

2 The leader must talk the partner through the obstacles but can only use the Celt compass to do so.

3 "Black" becomes straight ahead, "White" is backwards, "Purple" is right and "Pale" is left. "Dark Brown" is a little to the left and "Grey" is more to the left and so on.

4 The leader cannot use the word "Stop" (or left, right, ahead or back) but they can add the word "Cut-throat!" meaning "Stop!"

5 Score 10 for a clear run to the target; deduct a point for every obstacle touched.

6 Change the blindfold to the leader and try again. The winner is the one with the highest score as leader.

7 If there is more than one pair, then the pairs can race from one end of the room to the other. Touching any obstacle means the pair must go back to the start.

8 The winner is the pair to reach the far wall first. In the event of a tie the winner is the blindfolded partner with the fewest broken bones.

Sadly, the Celtic compass has died out. Otherwise we'd have had cowboys riding the range in the Wild Pale and polar bears at the Black Pole.

Manchester in the Grey of England (that sounds right) would be playing soccer against Pale Ham while you'd expect to see a lot of heather on the Purple coast of Scotland or buttercups in the Yellow part of Wales.

But what would we be eating two days after Good Friday? Purple-er eggs? Yeuch!

"DID YOU KNOW ...?
IN TRAVELLING IT IS CONSIDERED
UNLUCKY TO TRAVEL ANTI-
CLOCKWISE? THE SUPERSTITIOUS
CELTS ALWAYS MADE
SURE THEY TRAVELLED
IN THE SAME DIRECTION AS
THE SUN – CLOCKWISE OR
"DEOSIL" AS THEY CALLED IT.
WANT TO GET GOOD MARKS
IN THAT TEST? THEN
WALK ROUND THE

DESK DEOSIL BEFORE YOU SIT DOWN. WANT THAT HORRIBLE HISTORY TEACHER TO FALL OUT OF BED? WALK ROUND HIS CAR "WIDDERSHINS" (THAT'S ANTI-CLOCKWISE). REMEMBER THAT THE NUMBER THREE IS LUCKY FOR CELTS AND NINE (THAT'S THREE-THREES) IS MAGICAL. BUT WALKING ROUND THAT DESK NINE TIMES WOULD PROBABLY MAKE YOU TOO DIZZY TO SEE THE EXAM PAPER!"

Epilogue

Hopeless history

The Romans were horrible historians who tried to give the Celts a bad name. But for 1,500 years every other historian has repeated the same "fact"...

The Romans never reached Ireland

(Check your school history books and you're bound to find it there somewhere.)

How do the hopeless historians know the Romans never reached Ireland? Because the Romans never said they reached Ireland. This is not the same as the Romans saying they never reached Ireland.

And now the truth can be told at last...

THE ROMANS REACHED IRELAND

The history books are all wrong ... except this one, of course, but we don't like to boast!

THE HERALD

| BINGO! | WIN A CHAIR! | FREE RUBBISH! | MORE BINGO |

CELTIC MYTH DESTROYED

MYTH DESTROYED HERE!

A dull piece of land near Dublin holds the key to a Celtic mystery that has lasted for nearly 2,000 years. A team of archaeologists have announced that they've been investigating a 40-acre patch of ground about 15 miles north of Dublin. The spot, called Drumanagh, is the site of a Roman coastal fort. Earth walls and ditches show where the fort was – coins, ornaments and jewellery show that Romans lived there. Coins of emperors Titus, Trajan and Hadrian show the Romans lived in Ireland from at least AD 79 till AD 138 and historians never knew ... till now.

The fort has been described as the most important find in Irish history. But here's the really strange thing. The archaeologists knew the secret of the site in the 1980s and kept it hidden for over 10 years while they worked on it! Meanwhile thousands of children in hundreds of schools have been told, "The Romans never reached Ireland." Huh! Historians!

437

Could *you* keep the "most important find in Irish history" a secret for over 10 years? The coins and valuables went to the National Museum of Ireland where they were hidden away. The archaeologists, historians and museum staff hid the truth from us. It makes you wonder what else historians know that they won't tell us? Is Adolf Hitler still alive? Did King Arthur really exist? Did King Henry I have his brother murdered? Did Humpty Dumpty fall off the wall … or was he pushed?

STARTLING NEW EVIDENCE HAS COME TO LIGHT SUGGESTING THE BRICKS AT THE VERY TOP OF THE WALL MAY HAVE BEEN TAMPERED WITH

One day we may have answers to all of these questions…

The Celt comeback

The trouble with the Celts is they didn't bother to write much. So a lot of the things we hear about them were written by their enemies — people like the Romans. Would you trust *your* enemy to write good things about you?

Other things were written by people who did not approve of the Celts — people like the monks of the Middle Ages. The monks were Christian and the old Celts were not. You're not going to get a good school report from a teacher who doesn't approve of you!

Still the Roman writers seemed to respect these wild, strange people. Lucretius wrote…

AND THIS RACE OF PEOPLE FROM THE PLAINS WERE AS HARD AS THE HARD LAND THEY CAME FROM; THEY WERE BUILT ON FIRMER, STRONGER BONES AND GIVEN MIGHTY MUSCLES. THEY WERE A RACE UNAFRAID OF THE HEAT OR THE COLD, OF THE PLAGUE OR OF STRANGE FOODS. FOR MANY YEARS THEY LED THEIR LIVES AMONG THE BEASTS OF THE EARTH AND WERE NOT TAMED.

But the people who were "tamed" – the Romans – were able to defeat these heroic people. A Greek writer, Strabo, claimed that their fearless nature made them easy to outwit…

THE CELT RACE IS MADLY FOND OF WAR AND QUICK TO DO BATTLE. OTHERWISE THEY ARE HONEST AND NOT EVIL CHARACTERS. AND SO WHEN THEY ARE STIRRED UP THEY ASSEMBLE IN THEIR BANDS FOR BATTLE, QUITE OPENLY AND WITHOUT CAREFUL PLANNING. AS A RESULT THEY ARE EASILY HANDLED BY THOSE

WHO WANT TO OUTWIT THEM. FOR THE CELTS ARE ALWAYS READY TO FACE DANGER, EVEN IF THEY HAVE NOTHING ON THEIR SIDE BUT THEIR OWN STRENGTH AND COURAGE.

Strength and courage and honesty were not enough and as the years went by the Celts were driven back from the richest countries by enemies with more cunning and greed.

Of course, Strabo also pointed out that the Celts had some horrible historical habits...

THERE ARE ALSO OTHER ACCOUNTS OF THEIR HUMAN SACRIFICES; FOR THEY USED TO SHOOT MEN DOWN WITH ARROWS, OR MAKING A LARGE STATUE OF STRAW AND WOOD, THROW INTO IT CATTLE AND ALL SORTS OF WILD ANIMALS AND HUMAN BEINGS AND THUS MAKE A BURNT OFFERING.

BAAA BAAA

WOOF WOOF

But at least the Celts left behind many good things they made and we know they were great artists. They also left behind their ancestors who still live in Ireland, Scotland, Brittany (France) and Cornwall (England). And though the spiky, dyed hair is gone some of the mystic powers seem to remain in some of them.

It's sad that the cunning and greedy have taken the world from the honest and courageous. Maybe one day a leader will appear who will lead the world back to the ways of courage and honesty. Maybe his name will be … Arthur! It would be nice to think so. It's something to hope for, anyway.

CUT-THROAT CELTS

Quiz

It's a curious Celtic life...

So – reckon you know all about this terrible tribe, with all their curious customs and peculiar practices? Take this quick quiz and find out.

1 England was created when the Angles and the Saxons took over the south-east of Britain in AD 520. What did they call their new land?

a) Angle-land

b) Saxonia

c) Engal-land

2 What was the name of the largest Celt tribe that fought the Romans?

a) Celtics

b) Gauls

c) Zulus

3 Why did the Celts cut off people's heads in battle?
a) They believed that they gained their enemy's wisdom and strength
b) They wanted to look down their enemy's throats
c) They wanted to eat them

4 Kissing under the mistletoe is a Celtic tradition, but the Celts only believed the mistletoe was magical when…
a) It was cut on the first day of July under a full moon
b) It was cut by a Druid using a gold sickle
c) It was plucked from a bough by a magpie

5 The Celts believed that the Druids had magical powers, but which of the following was not a Druid power?

a) Changing the weather
b) Time-travelling
c) Flying

> MMM, I THINK I'LL GO BACK 5 MINUTES AND HAVE THAT CAKE ALL OVER AGAIN

6 The Celts believed in sacrificing people to keep their gods happy. How was the practice of "death by air" carried out?

a) The victim was suffocated
b) The victim was strangled
c) The victim was hung

7 The first Celts lived during the Iron Age. What did this mean?

a) They were good at getting the creases out of their favourite tunics

b) They used iron for making tools and weapons

c) They used iron bars for money

8 If you were round at a Celt's house and you smelled cedar oil coming from a chest, what would you find inside?

a) Nice-smelling blankets

b) Christmas presents

c) Heads

Bonkers beliefs

The Celts were a crazy bunch. If you met one on the street and they told you the following facts, would you believe them? See if you can tell the troublesome truth from the foolish fiction.

1 "I've just thrown my favourite sheep off the cliff so the gods will bless me with more sheep."

2 "Can't stop. I'm off to get my nails done."

3 "My best friend just died, so I'm off round his place for a good cry."

4 "Would you mind holding my clothes while I nip off and fight a battle?"

5 "Hang on … Just remembered. I'm not fighting today – I spotted a crane earlier."

6 "We've spent all year growing corn, and now that we've harvested it we're going to bury it."

7 "I'm off to help St Brannoc build a church because he found a cow and her calf there – and that's magic he says."

8 "I've just turned sixteen so I've been turfed out of me mum and dad's and made to live with another family."

Could you be a Celt?

Now you've found out all about Celts, how do you think you'd fare in the evil Iron Age? Take this quiz and find out if the Celts would welcome you as a warrior or sacrifice you by suffocation…

1 The Celts bathed every day, but would you be able to play with your rubber duck in peace? (Clue: It's a family affair)

2 You know all about Halloween, of course, but what would you do on 31 October if you were a Celt? (Clue: It's not a trick question)

3 If you were a Celtic sailor, what do you think would keep you from drowning? (Clue: A bird in the hand…)

4 If you were involved in a game of hurling with some ancient warriors, what would you use as a ball? (Clue: Use your head!)

5 You'd have to learn to fight fiercely, but who'd be teaching you? (Clue: Dress-ed to kill)

6 The Celts were good at finding their way around. They used a compass with colours to show direction. If you were off in a purple direction, which way would you be heading? (Clue: Into the sunrise)

HOW WAS I TO KNOW HE WAS COLOUR BLIND?

455

7 Playing apple-bobbing on Halloween, you see a girl stick the apple pips on her face. What on Earth is she doing? (Clue: It's a horrible husband Halloween habit)

8 If a Celtic woman asked you to pick her up some make-up, where would you go? (Clue: It's a berry simple question…)

Answers

It's a curious Celtic life...

1a) They called it Angle-land, which eventually became England.

2b) Roman Ammianus Marcellinus noted that the Gauls were fierce, argued a lot and were proud.

3a) They believed that a person's power was all in their head – even if they were dead!

4b) They believed that the oak tree was holy and the mistletoe that grew on it had magical powers.

5c) Druids could also (they said) change their shape to anything they wanted and bring down mists to make themselves invisible ... but they couldn't fly.

6a, **b** or **c)** Sacrificing to the God of air was carried out by suffocation, as well as hanging and strangulation.

7b) Iron was the magnificent metal of this era and was used for all sorts of things – tools, pots, jewellery – you name it.

8c) The Celts liked to keep heads as trophies, and would preserve them in cedar oil.

Bonkers beliefs

1 True – the Celts believed that by sacrificing animals the gods would look favourably on them.

2 True – wealthy Celts were big on manicures!

3 False – when somebody died the Celts threw a big party and had a right old laugh!

4 True – the Celts often fought naked, probably to scare their opponents. Not the wisest thing to do in the winter…

5 True – seeing a crane (the bird not the lifting machine) was unlucky, they thought, and Celtic warriors used it as an excuse to pack up and go home!

459

I'M *DEFINITELY* NOT FIGHTING TODAY!

6 Totally true — it seems like a daft idea, but placing the grain in the ground it kept it fresh until it was needed.

7 Almost true — St B built a church on the site where he found a sow and her piglets, not a cow. He was told to build it in a dream.

8 False — he would have been moved out at the age of seven! This was meant to teach Celtic kids that they were part of a tribe, not just a family.

Could you be a Celt?

1 Not a chance. Better hope you were part of a small family as you'd all have to share your time in the tub.

2 You'd dress in a scary costume to ward off the spirits. No trick or treating, though.

3 A feather from a wren – especially if the feather had come from a bird that had been killed on New Year's Day.

4 Chances are you'd be throwing round the head of one of your enemies. Don't try this at school...

5 A woman – the men were too busy so the women taught fighting.

6 You'd be heading east (as long as you weren't colour blind).

7 She'd be trying to find out the name of her future husband. She'd name each of the pips and the last to fall off would be the name of the person she was going to marry.

8 No – not the local supermarket! You'd go to the woods. The juice from herbs and berries was used as make-up.

Interesting Index

mouse brains, in toothpaste 194
murder 145, 186–7, 288, 333, 334, 342, 418
    by Roman emperors 93, 94, 99, 106
    of Roman emperors 7, 12, 14, 75, 101, 104, 105, 106, 217
murder trials 410–13

necks 217, 294–5, 318
    chalk on 279
    chopping 218, 349
    see also heads, cutting off; throats, cutting
Nennius (Welsh monk) 307–8
Nero (Roman emperor) 93–100, 104, 145, 225, 298
nightmares 78
North Africa 10, 239

Octavia (Nero's wife) 94
Octavian (Caesar's nephew) 82
Olympus, Mount 121

ostrich brains 162, 229
Otherworld (Celt afterlife) 289, 346, 391, 416 see also afterlife

pagans 190, 210, 307
Parisii (Yorkshire tribe) 328
parties, wild 92
Patrick (patron saint) 189–91, 244, 286
Paulinus, Suetonius (Roman general) 13, 101, 337
pease pudding 372–3
Penates (god) 173
Persia 178
Pertinax (Roman emperor) 104
Philippi, battle of 82
Picts (Scottish tribe) 13, 184, 202, 211, 242, 385, 392, 394–5
pigs 163, 318, 376–7, 460
    bladders 132–3
pirates 189
plagues 287, 440
plays, violent 152–3
Pliny (Roman historian) 369
Plutarch (Roman writer) 79, 217

473

476